Management for Research in U.S. Universities

Raymond J. Woodrow

National Association of College and University Business Officers
WASHINGTON, D.C.

Copyright © 1978 by the National Association
   of College and University Business Officers
One Dupont Circle
Washington, D.C. 20036

All rights reserved
Printed in the United States of America
Edited and designed by Abbott Wainwright

Library of Congress Cataloging in Publication Data

   Woodrow, Raymond J
      Management for research in U.S. universities.

      1. Research—United States—Management.
   2. Universities and colleges—United States.
   I. Title.
   Q180.U5W63   658'.91'00143   77-27085
   ISBN 0-915164-05-1

*Management for Research
in U.S. Universities*

Contents

	Foreword	vii
	Preface	ix
	Introduction	xiii
1	The Climate for Research	1
2	Policies and Criteria	13
3	Developing and Implementing Sponsored Research	21
4	Interdisciplinary Research	33
5	Professional Personnel Other than Faculty	43
6	Patents and Copyrights	51
7	Indirect Costs	65
8	Administrative Offices and Supporting Services and Facilities	81
9	Organization	93
10	A Preferred System of Management for Research	103

Foreword

THE PRIMARY FUNCTIONS OF THE UNIVERSITY HAVE TRADITIONALLY been labeled as instruction, research, and public service; in the academic structure, these are generally inseparable. The present volume sets the research function apart (as much as it is possible to do so) in order to suggest how the activities that support research may be tailored to provide an environment in which research can thrive.

The welfare of the nation, and perhaps the world, may be critically influenced by the quality of research performed in U.S. universities, although we may be reminded of this only when Nobel prizes are awarded or when a vaccine is developed or when a research effort such as DNA is subjected to public discussion. Such items as these that reach the news can scarcely indicate the scope, nature, or quality of the total research effort being carried out in universities. Each sound research project, insignificant though it may seem, adds some increment to the body of knowledge and, it is hoped, to the world's betterment.

Ray Woodrow has had a notable career in university research. The latest milestone was marked on October 12, 1977, when he received the Distinguished Contribution to Research Administration Award from the Society of Research Administrators; his name and contributions were placed in nomination by William G. Bowen, president of Princeton University.

The author's insights, set out here, should provide food for thought to those concerned with research in our universities. He speaks to sponsoring agencies such as the federal government and private foundations, to governing boards, and to university administrators; his remarks are often critical, and some of his suggestions will be unacceptable to one or more of these groups. In any event, this book should stimulate discussions addressing management for research to bring about improved practices for both the universities and the agencies that sponsor the research they perform.

As with all NACUBO publications carrying an author's name, the views expressed are those of the author, and publication does not signify acceptance or endorsement by the association.

D. F. FINN
Executive Vice President
NACUBO

Preface

THIS BOOK IS BASED ON MY THIRTY-FIVE YEARS OF INVOLVEMENT WITH research in universities. During World War II, I spent three years at the Office of Scientific Research and Development, the first government agency to utilize in any broad sense the research capabilities of universities. This period was followed by two years at the MIT Radiation Laboratory, where I worked with many scientists and engineers as the associate project engineer of the largest wartime radar project.

After the war, Princeton University opened the door to a brand new kind of career. Starting as executive officer and secretary of a Committee on Project Research and Inventions, and graduating later to other titles, I became intimately involved with practically every aspect of management for research that is covered in this volume, except for those aspects peculiar to state universities. In most cases new ground was being broken; there were no precedents anywhere. An occasional false start has proved to be as instructive for the purposes of writing this book as for the many more correct paths taken.

However, much more than Princeton University is involved. In 1948 I was associate secretary and principal author for the "Report of the Committee on Contractual and Administrative Procedures for Research and Development in the Department of the Army"; that report was a forerunner of the present Armed Services Procurement Regulations and later Federal Procurement Regulations, which are the backbone of government contracts today. In the 1950s and 1960s, eight years as chairman of the Committee on Relations with the Federal Government of the Engineering College Research Council and two years as chairman of the Council itself brought wide knowledge of research organizations and practices in engineering colleges. For ten consecutive years in the 1960s and 1970s I was a member of the Committee on Governmental Relations of the National Association of College and University Business Officers, which provided wide exposure to business and research administration affairs in many universities and to their relations with government. Membership in the National Council of University Research Administrators since its inception, including chairman for one term, and membership in the Society of

PREFACE

Research Administrators have provided additional exposure to various aspects of management for research.

As a member of the Committee on Sponsored Projects of the American Council on Education in the late 1960s, I cooperated in the supervision and preparation of the well-used volume *Sponsored Research in American Universities and Colleges*. Presidency of the Society of University Patent Administrators has presented me with in-depth access to patent and copyright policies and practices. I have been, in addition, an adviser or consultant to a number of institutions on problems of management for research.

Notwithstanding these experiences, this book would probably not have been written had it not been for a grant awarded to Princeton University in 1974 by the Research Management Improvement Program of the National Science Foundation (NSF grant NM42893). This grant provided for my visiting 33 universities that had stated, in response to an NSF inquiry, that they would appreciate advice and assistance on various aspects of research management. The universities to which the inquiry was addressed were all of those having research expenditures funded by the federal government in amounts between $4 million and $13 million a year, although the vagaries of research expenditure reporting resulted in the inclusion of several institutions with much larger amounts. When all the favorable replies to the inquiry had been analyzed, the topics of interest to one or more universities could be segregated under thirteen headings. To some extent the chapter titles in this volume parallel those headings, with certain condensations.

Performance under the NSF grant involved visits to all 33 institutions after they had outlined in a letter their topics of interest and had included copies of pertinent statements of policies and practices. A visit took from two to four days at each institution, where I engaged in discussions with academic, business, and research administration officers plus several principal investigators, sometimes up to ten. A written report with recommendations was furnished in each case to supplement or summarize the discussions.

Following the 33 visits, four major research universities were visited in connection with an NSF grant to the Association of American Universities for a study of the future role of research in universities (NSF grant PRM75-17417A01). By this time the chapter outline for this book had been developed, which could serve as the basis for discussions, whereas in the earlier visits the objective was to provide advice and assistance on only those topics of concern to the university being visited. When all visits had been completed under both grants, I prepared an abbreviated version of what has now become this volume and sent it to each university for comment. The replies were helpful and encouraging.

Because of the nature of some of the information provided under these two projects, and because of assurances given, none of the facts, information, or impressions gathered are attributed to any university; the sole exception to this rule is that information about Princeton University is used in several instances. Only a few specific references are cited; there are many publications that have influenced my thoughts and actions over the years, and to list them all would be futile. I alone am responsible for what is said in this book, but must at the same time express my deep appreciation to everyone who has contributed either knowingly or unknowingly to this enterprise for improving management for research in universities.

This volume is not a textbook; it is an attempt to set forth my views with regard to certain aspects of management for research that have been of concern to persons at various levels of mangement in many universities. Some will disagree with these views, but I hope that more will agree, and that what is presented will be helpful.

Introduction

UNIVERSITY MANAGEMENT *FOR* RESEARCH, NOT *OF* RESEARCH, IS THE SUBject of this book. The difference between these terms is not merely symbolic. Management for research, as discussed in the pages that follow, covers primarily the provision of a nourishing climate, sound policies, supporting services of various kinds, financial systems, and organizational arrangements that will help research to flourish in a university. This volume covers topics much broader than research administration, since it ranges from state legislatures through professional research personnel to university-wide organizations for research. But throughout, as the title implies, the purpose is primarily to counsel with regard to management that will facilitate research rather than direct it.

The management of research, in the sense that management means to direct as industry directs for limited corporate purposes or as government directs to achieve a governmental mission, is rare in a university environment. That sort of management or direction is generally left in the university to principal investigators, sometimes called project directors or project managers, who are generally members of the faculty. It is their endeavors that the climate, the policies, and the supporting services provided by management for research are meant largely to assist.

Some research is performed in some universities in spite of inadequate or poor management support. Dedicated persons of ability perform research under almost any circumstances. On the other hand, they may not stay long, or they may not come in the first place, if management is deficient. To the extent that they do come and stay, their research is hampered and performance degraded by poor management support.

There are other aspects of what can be called university management that this book does not cover. No one can generalize with omniscience about the appropriate balance between research and instruction in all universities. The types of research an institution should foster, and to what extent, are peculiar to each. And the percentage of an institution's funds that should be devoted to its own research or to cost sharing in sponsored research, although some aspects are discussed in this volume, is still a subject for institution-by-institution decision.

1

The Climate for Research

A UNIVERSITY HAS UNDOUBTEDLY BEEN DEFINED SOMEWHERE AS A COMmunity of scholars primarily devoted to the education of students and the advancement of knowledge. Research has as its goal the advancement of knowledge. *Advances in knowledge are the rungs in the ladder for the ascent of man.* The knowledge that is the product of research today becomes the subject matter of what is taught tomorrow. As knowledge gained and then learned diffuses through civilized humanity, it may be put to use in its pristine form, but it is more likely to be used in combination with other old and new knowledge so that its identity is obscured or completely lost. Tracing a new sprig of knowledge to its ultimate use can be as difficult as tracing one's ancestry to Adam and Eve.

The name "university" carries with it a strong implication that research for the advancement of knowledge is a *major* function of an institution that calls itself a university. Granting of the Ph.D. degree requires research resulting in a dissertation or thesis that constitutes a contribution to knowledge. In 1974 about 33,000 Ph.D.s were awarded in the United States by universities performing about $3 billion of research (excluding federally funded research and development centers), or nearly $100,000 on the average for each Ph.D. awarded (data from the Association of Graduate Schools and the National Science Foundation). This is not meant to say that every Ph.D. on the average required that much research, since a significant amount of university research involves no graduate students. It does mean that a university, or a state that has established a university, has made a strong moral and intrinsic commitment to provide a satisfactory climate for research if that university awards the Ph.D.

However, the commitment to research for many universities is much broader and deeper than for the single purpose of granting degrees. To those institutions, the advancement of knowledge, i.e., the fabrication of steps in the ladder for the ascent of man, is the essential objective apart from the education of students. A truly nourishing climate for research is then also essential, in the sense that the term "climate for research" is used here.

Providing the right climate does not imply that an institution must pay

MANAGEMENT FOR RESEARCH

from its own resources (or from the state's resources in a state institution) for all research carried on. Certainly it should pay for some, as discussed later in this chapter, but nearly 90% of all research carried on by universities in the aggregate is "sponsored" by outside sources of funds such as the federal government, state agencies, private foundations, voluntary health agencies, and industry. In many ways this sponsored research imposes more rigorous demands on the climate and management for research than does internally financed research. Because such a great majority of research in universities is externally sponsored, a large part of this chapter and this book has been written with that fact in mind.

The climate for research involves a variety of people, policies, practices, and attitudes that have a widespread effect on research in a university and on the university itself. Other, more concentrated topics are the subject matter for later chapters.

Governing Bodies

State governments for state universities and governing boards for both state and independent universities play an important role in determining the sort of climate that exists for research. They affect the management for research in various ways and, in fact, are part of that management.

The role of governing boards in independent universities is not easily identified when one looks at research. Such boards concern themselves with financial aspects, including the adequacy of reimbursements for the costs incurred on sponsored research. They may become involved in undertaking or continuing large laboratories like federally financed research and development centers (FFRDCs). They may express concern over the relation between teaching and research. Their approval of a university budget is definitely important, particularly if an allocation of any significance explicitly for research and paid for from the university's unrestricted funds appears in such a budget. The board's choice of a president may set a trend as to university attitudes toward research. However, boards rarely tamper with details of management, or what they consider to be details.

Concerning state universities, there is almost a complete disparity between those that have constitutional status and those that do not. Institutions not having constitutional status, and they are in the majority, are often subject to line-item control of budgets, mandated standards for faculty teaching loads, civil service requirements for many nonfaculty positions, purchasing and subcontracting through a state purchasing system, integration of accounting with a state accounting system, and more. Most of these factors are discussed in greater detail later in this volume. Each one is usually damaging to the climate for research in a university because research is a special sort of enterprise, namely, exploring the *unknown*. Other parts of a university and of a state government are generally concerned with what is *known*. Exploration of the unknown must operate under more flexible rules and regulations than pursuits whose courses are reasonably predictable. *Sponsored* research can be even more heavily affected by onerous state regulations because there may be conflicting requirements between the sponsor and the state. It is for these reasons that a number of state universities have established affiliated foundations to handle many of the functions necessary to conduct quality research. Other universities have struggled along without such foundations, but have been clearly handicapped. For the reasons stated, as will later be amplified, *a more enlightened state attitude would be a major step in improving the climate for research.*

State universities having constitutional status seem to have few of the problems enumerated above; in many ways, they function like independent universities. State universities ranking near the top in annual research expenditures generally fall in this category. However, for reasons that seem quite apart from research, there are state universities of this type whose legislatures are endeavoring to obtain substantially more control. Though not aimed at research, such controls could impair the performance of research.

Principal Officers

The principal officers of universities that are dedicated to the advancement of knowledge as a primary objective need to believe strongly in the importance of research and to contend for its existence. They should understand the processes by which research is done, if not its subject matter. An understanding of the attitudes and intellectual objectives of those who perform research can be of significant value.

The leadership needed in university presidents and other principal officers is a quality hard to define. However, one can detect, if not prove, from the sentiments expressed down on the "firing line" whether there is real or only lip-service priority given to research. Time off from presiding over "affairs of state" to visit research laboratories and centers, including time to discuss problems with researchers, is highly beneficial in both directions; the word spreads that there is high-level interest in what is going on.

Words and action are both important. *Words* taking the form of convincing presentations based on strong beliefs are particularly important if governing bodies such as state legislatures are to be convinced that the advancement of knowledge is significant in more ways than can be immediately foreseen for the improvement of agriculture or the utilization of coal, for example. *Action* provides the funds, facilities, and procedures needed for research to the extent that these can be controlled at the university level. A university president can play a major role in affecting the factors of the climate for research discussed later in this chapter. The combination of words and action can help to provide the reputation that is so important in attracting funds for research from outside sources, both government and private; there are no substitutes.

Finally, in areas affecting research, the principal officers of universities sometimes ignore the sound management precepts of employing the most competent persons for the jobs to be done, rewarding them as well as possible, and delegating authority *and* responsibility to the fullest extent possible. The status in the university hierarchy of the senior person responsible for research-related matters has a significant effect not only internally but also in commanding respect in external relations.

Department Chairmen

In addition to the principal officers of an institution, department chairmen play a key role in advancing the caliber and size of research within their departments. They can play an important part in the appointment, advancement in salary, and promotion of research-oriented faculty. Where a reduced teaching schedule on a departmental basis has been observed, thus freeing time for research, the department chairman was primarily responsible. Department chairmen can fight for and obtain facilities and funding, they can set an example by conducting research themselves, and they can help build a departmental tradition that will last for a long time.

Research Emphasis in Appointments, Advancement, and Promotions

The emphasis on research potential and research performance in appointing, advancing, and promoting faculty has an obvious and major effect on the climate for research in a university. This does not necessarily mean an all-out emphasis on "publish or perish." It does mean careful consideration of evaluations made of research potential and performance by others in the same discipline and, within that discipline, by others in the same specialty. Since not enough evaluations (sometimes not even any) can be made within the institution, major research universities make it a practice to get them from outside "peers." Universities less eminent in research often do not follow this practice, or sometimes follow it only in departments that have elected on their own to adopt it.

In view of the importance of research qualifications for those who will be principal investigators, universities that aspire to improving their research potential should take every measure possible, including the peer review system, to recruit, advance, and promote persons having those qualifications. This should be true for all schools in a university where research is important.

Teaching Loads

At major research institutions, teaching loads of research faculty members (generally measured in class contact hours) usually average six hours or less per week. This means that, when administrative duties, committee work, and other responsibilities are taken into consideration, about 25% to 50% of a faculty member's time is available for research. Not only does this create the climate for research for faculty members who are already on the staff, but it is the strongest kind of inducement for attracting new faculty who have a real interest in research.

By comparison, many of the medium to smaller research universities ("medium to smaller" in this volume refers to the size of university research programs, not to the size of the universities themselves) have teaching loads of as much as twelve hours or more a week. In state universities, teaching loads are often mandated by the legislature. After the addition of administrative, committee, and other duties (which some state legislatures refuse to recognize), the amount of time (and energy) left for research is minimal unless a faculty member consistently works long hours. For institutions attempting a bootstrap operation to improve research stature, reduced teaching schedules for faculty members having research potential do yield some results, but the climate for attracting new faculty with strong interests in research will not thereby be much improved. Such selective treatment for research-oriented faculty is certain to have effects on the morale of other faculty if the salaries paid are all from the same source of funds.

Universities that have a goal of becoming distinguished for research should have a parallel goal of teaching loads that provide a substantial amount of faculty time for research. This latter goal is not one that can be reached either easily or quickly. There may be many faculty with neither interest in nor qualifications for genuine research so that reduced teaching loads may have to be instituted on a selective basis; this has been done with some success on a departmental basis. A rather drastic alternative has been observed, with most research being conducted in institutes staffed primarily with researchers who are not regular members of the faculty.

Charging Faculty Time to Research

Practices with regard to the charging of faculty time to research during the academic year, particularly sponsored research, vary widely among universities and even among departments in the same university. There is a much greater correlation within the same discipline in a variety of universities than there is among different disciplines in the same university. In the natural sciences, for example, there is much less charging of faculty time to research during the academic year than there is in engineering or medicine. When charging is done, some institutions base the charge on the time released from normal teaching and administrative duties, while others charge to the extent that effort is devoted to a project without regard to any released time. (Incidentally, some would make a distinction between "time" and "effort," but to the author it seems that unless one works on a piecework basis, the only method for measuring effort is time.)

There seem to be many reasons for the differences in charging for faculty effort during the academic year, including departmental or discipline traditions, prejudices as to source of salary, fears of possible consequences of direct charges, dogmas that cannot be changed, pecuniary consequences, and probably many more. In a line-budgeting system, part of a professor's salary that is removed for charging to sponsored research may be difficult to reinstate later. Sections within sponsoring agencies awarding grants or contracts for research in a particular discipline may affect an entire discipline with regard to this one factor.

Notwithstanding the variations in practice, and the reasons for these variations, they do *not* appear to have a significant effect on the climate for research. Major research universities are as apt as any other universities to charge faculty salaries to sponsored research. However, institutions with heavy teaching loads are and will be severely hampered in building research by restrictive practices of sponsors. Private foundations that look unkindly on paying part of a professor's salary for work on a grant are in this respect like government sponsors with similar attitudes.

Institutional Funds for Research

It was stated earlier that nearly 90% of the funds spent on research in universities in the aggregate come from outside sponsors. This figure and others cited in this section are based on a report issued annually by the National Science Foundation. According to table B-18 of the 1976 report, about $3.7 billion were spent on research (including a tiny amount on development) in colleges and universities, excluding federally funded research and development centers such as the Jet Propulsion Laboratory, Los Alamos, etc., and *also* excluding research not separately budgeted and accounted for but instead included in regular departmental instruction budgets.* Eleven and a half percent of the total expenditures of about $3.7 billion, a percentage that has been relatively constant during recent years, is the amount institutions reported spending on research from funds that they were free to designate for this purpose. The sources of institutional or so-called "free" funds for research include unrestricted or general-purpose endowment income, state and local government appropriations, unrestricted or general-purpose grants and gifts from outside sources, and tuition and fees.

These internally available funds for research are important to universities. The case has been made to state legislatures and private donors by many institutions that such funds are important for university survival. The case has also been made that government regulations should provide for an allowance for "independent research and development" in the indirect cost rates for grants and contracts to universities, similar to an allowance granted for many years to industry.

The reasons for needing such funds include:

1. To lay a foundation of research experience, expertise, and knowledge in areas where there may ultimately be sponsor interest.

2. To fund research involving new concepts that are too radical for a sponsor to accept today.

3. To fund young researchers who have not yet achieved the stature to succeed in obtaining outside support.

4. To carry forward research too inexpensive to justify the costs and delays involved in a proposal and ultimate grant or contract.

5. To perform preliminary research that may be essential in preparing a convincing proposal.

6. To carry on research that is clearly an advancement of knowledge, but that is not now but possibly some day may be of interest to an outside sponsor.

---

* "Expenditures for Scientific Activities at Universities and Colleges, Fiscal Year 1976—Detailed Statistical Tables," NSF77-316, (Washington, D.C.: National Science Foundation, 1977), Appendices B and C.

These are convincing reasons, but let us return to the data. Based on the author's observations, there are sizable inconsistencies in the amounts of internally available funds reported by some institutions. However, from a statistical point of view, the averages certainly convey some meaning. As mentioned above, for all universities, 11.5% of the total funds spent on research come from institutional sources. The corresponding percentage for the top 20 universities ranked in order of research-dollar volume was 10.1%, which means that universities with a smaller research volume spent roughly the same as the top-ranking institutions. In public (state and local government) universities the percentage was 14.7%, whereas in independent universities the percentage dropped far down to 5.8%.

However, there is an explanation that probably accounts for part, possibly a large part, of the higher percentage of institutional funds for research in state as compared with independent universities. In chapter 7, under the heading "Use of Indirect Cost Reimbursements," there is discussion of the practice in many state universities of *ostensibly* using part of the reimbursement from sponsors for the indirect costs of sponsored projects as a method of financing internal research, among other uses. This rarely happens in independent universities. The advantage that state universities enjoy may be due in part to these *ostensible* indirect cost funds that are used for internal research.

With regard to the data that show the top-ranking research universities, both public and independent, actually spending a bit less (on a percentage basis) on internal research than do lower-ranking institutions, it must be remembered that the NSF data include only research separately budgeted and accounted for. The higher-ranking universities, as explained earlier in this chapter, generally have lower faculty teaching loads, and thus greater time for research. The salaries for the time involved in this additional research, plus applicable indirect costs and undoubtedly other expenditures as well, are included in regular instruction and departmental research budgets and are not measured in the NSF data because they are not separately budgeted and accounted for. If these unmeasured expenditures for research were added to the actual research expenditures reported, the major research universities would almost certainly be at the top of the list in percentage of institutional funds for research.

Basic versus Applied Research

There have been many attempts to define basic and applied research, so no such attempt will be made here. The problem seems to be that there is no *intrinsic quality* that can be used as the basis for distinction. As a result, the motivation of the researcher, the mission of the sponsor, or the eye of the beholder are used to make the distinction. Practically all advances in knowledge, which are the results of research, are put to use or "applied" sooner or later. In this sense all research is ultimately "applicable," which is the term that some would substitute for "applied." Of course, some of what is called applied research is not research at all, but merely a reclassification of knowledge that is already available.

National Science Foundation surveys and reports stress data on basic research; many universities emphasize it in their written or unwritten policies. Some university scientists shy away from the performance of research whose results might be used. An aeronautical engineering department chairman reports that the research in his department is 100% basic, which would greatly surprise sponsors in the Department of Defense and the National Aeronautics and Space Administration. Colleagues in the mathematics department would describe the same research as 100% applied. Whose view is right? There are no known reports on total support of basic versus applied research by government agencies, but if there were, one would be hard put to believe that the data reported were for the same research that the universities reported on.

If one looks for a realistic approach to the basic versus applied problem—an approach that does not rely on motivation, mission, or the eye of the beholder, but on measurable, intrinsic qualities—one might accept a continuous spectrum from research where there is no effort or attention paid to application, but only the advancement of knowledge, to the other end at which there is no research for the advancement of knowledge, and all effort is devoted to application. From one end of the spectrum to the other, the percentage of what can rightfully be called basic research decreases and the percentage of application grows. In this approach, there is no applied research; there is research and there is application, though both may exist at the same time in the same project.

To sum up this exercise, universities need to remember that research as research is for the advancement of knowledge, and that the application of knowledge is something different. Scorn for certain types of research because someone can visualize an application for the results is unwarranted. Criticisms of governmental support of very specific applied research might better be aimed at the breadth or the subject matter of the projects in which advances in knowledge are sought. Or, more appropriately in many cases, criticism might be leveled at projects called research in which much of the work is actually application and not research at all.

For Value Received

Many members of the faculty and administration regard contracts and grants for research received by their universities as gifts or even as charitable contributions to be used for the sole benefit of the institution. In some cases this may be true, but in the vast majority of cases it is not true, and there is a clear expectation by the sponsor that something of value will be performed and delivered in return for the funds provided.

For contracts or contractual-type agreements from the government, there should be little argument with the proposition that something of value is expected to be performed and delivered in return for the funds provided. However, as not so widely accepted, the same is also true for government *grants* for research. The U.S. Comptroller General has ruled that "the acceptance of a grant creates a contract between the United States and the Grantee" (42 Comp. Gen. 289, 294 (1962)). When Congress appropriates funds for research to the various government agencies, it does so not for the benefit of the institutions that will receive research grants as a result, but rather for the benefit of the nation's welfare. The government need not be the direct user of the research results, since it is the people the government represents who are expected to be the beneficiaries in areas such as health and welfare, clean environment, food and lodging, or just greater knowledge that may serve as a step in the ladder for the ascent of man.

The concept that government funds for research are a gift or charitable contribution and not a payment for the performance and delivery of something of value has led and will continue to lead to all sorts of problems. The deplorable requirement that the recipients of government research grants must share the costs of performance is a direct outgrowth of the philosophy underlying charitable contributions. Pressures for geographic distribution without regard to merit or value are another result. Perhaps most damaging, and subtly so, are internal university beliefs that performance is not important and that merely being a member of University X or Y should almost automatically result in grants being made available.

Research grants from private organizations such as foundations and voluntary health agencies should be looked at in much the same way as government grants; however, there is seldom the quid pro quo as in government grants or contracts, where the government is the user of results. But there is the need, imposed by charter or statute or both, that something of value be expected from the expenditure of funds for purposes such as new knowledge for the health, welfare, or education of mankind.

Of course, what has been said above does not necessarily apply to either government or private grants or contracts that are for purposes other than or broader than research.

Entrepreneurs and Loyalties

A phenomenon during the booming years of government funds for university research, which occurred at about the same time that universities were expanding, was the almost peripatetic scientist of some renown moving from campus to campus, taking along his or her grants and contracts. The leveling off of government funds and the absence of growth, if not an actual decline, in university staffing seem to have significantly deflated the phenomenon, but it still exists.

A key reason for this phenomenon, which has been stated many times, is that loyalties are more to disciplines than they are to institutions. Another important reason, perhaps even more important, is that university managements do not manage university research. The real managers are the principal investigators, who are the entrepreneurs in the business of research. Their enterprises are generally more self-contained and their relations with sponsors are often more personal than is true for those in industrial organizations. Thus, pulling up stakes and moving is easier in a university.

The matter of university researchers as entrepreneurs recurs throughout this volume, either implicitly or explicitly. They are apt to resist university policies for research, as discussed in chapter 2. They are the keys to development of proposals, often to the solicitation of funds, and obviously to the performance of research, as discussed in chapter 3. Lack of accommodation to team effort is a factor in interdisciplinary research, as discussed in chapter 4. Emphasis on direct charging of research costs under their control is a factor in determining direct and indirect costs in chapter 7. And centralized versus decentralized shops, stockrooms, and computers have a bearing, as discussed in chapter 8.

From a holistic point of view, a university should be greater than the sum of its material and human parts. However, this is probably not true if the parts are tied together only by threads. The combination of researchers, entrepreneurial initiatives, loyalties, and university requires an unusual adhesive. Providing that adhesive must be in large part the task of management for research.

2

Policies and Criteria

ALL UNIVERSITIES CAN BE SAID TO HAVE POLICIES AND CRITERIA governing the research they will undertake. Some of these are spelled out rather completely in written documents widely distributed, some are partly in writing and partly understood, and some are not written at all. The absence of any policies or criteria is occasionally found and this absence is in itself a policy.

Many policies and criteria for research are directed primarily to *sponsored* research, and a large majority of the issues discussed in this book arise only, or arise to any significant degree, in the area of sponsored research. Furthermore, as evidenced by the data in chapter 1, sponsored research constitutes about 90% of all the separately budgeted and identifiable research that is carried on in universities.

The following statement, which most universities would subscribe to, although probably in different words, appears as a preamble in the Princeton University statement of policies for sponsored research:

"Princeton University has based its adoption of these policies for sponsored research upon the fact that it is dedicated to the following primary and essential objectives:

- The education of undergraduate, graduate, and postdoctoral students.
- The advancement of knowledge through research and scholarship.
- The preservation and dissemination of knowledge.
- The advancement and protection of the public interest and public welfare."

The disadvantages of having written policies and criteria are that they are difficult to formulate with wide acceptance and that they can become too cumbersome or restrictive. To some persons, "academic freedom" should not be tied down by policies, no matter what the purposes of those policies may be.

However, the advantages of written policies and criteria, if they are carefully prepared and widely endorsed, as by a full faculty or a faculty senate, give concrete evidence of a university's intention to have the research performed contribute to the university's objectives (such as the

Princeton objectives cited above). Universities that have such policies and criteria have the "feel" of being better managed than those that do not. Wide internal availability of such policies and criteria can serve as guidelines to faculty and staff concerning the kinds of endeavor called "research" that will or will not be acceptable. They can help to avoid preparation of proposals and preliminary negotiations for projects that will not be accepted. Finally, they can serve as a beacon to everyone both inside and outside the university as to what the university stands for.

It is thus important to have well considered and widely endorsed written policies and criteria for sponsored research, but a mechanism for exceptions based on high-level review is desirable. The subjects to be covered in a written statement of policies and criteria are discussed in the remainder of this chapter. Conclusions reached as to each subject are those of the author alone, but every university considering the adoption or revision of a statement of policies and criteria should weigh each subject in the process.

Advancement of Knowledge

Should all of what a university does under the term "research" be for the purpose of advancing knowledge? If it is properly defined as "research," whether it is called "basic" or "applied," it will almost certainly contribute to the advancement of knowledge. Whether the use to which the hoped-for knowledge will be put is apparent or is conjectural ought to have little bearing on whether research will be undertaken. However, based on the discussion in chapter 1, projects that contain too much application of knowledge and not much advancement of knowledge may be seriously questioned. Product development, routine testing, service operations, and the like are not properly research at all; they do not embrace activities that can be used for a student's thesis or dissertation, and they rarely provide the new knowledge that, in the future, can be taught. If such activities are carried on as a public service, which is more likely in a state institution, they ought not to be exalted with the appellation of research, and their acceptance should be governed by separate policies and criteria.

Outside Direction or Control

Outside direction or control refers to any provisions in a grant or contract that give an outside sponsor a continuing unilateral voice in how research is performed or in the direction it should take. A university has no way of avoiding the inherent outside direction or control resulting from a sponsor's determination of what research will be funded or what will not, except by refusing to undertake the kinds of research funding offered.

However, once a contract or grant has been received, mechanisms for the exertion of outside direction or control are most often contained in specific contract provisions from government and also from industry, or otherwise through the use of "changes" provisions, which give the sponsor the right to make changes.

Some universities are adamantly opposed to any form of outside direction or control, insisting that the original description on the basis of which the grant or contract was awarded, with *mutual agreement* as to any subsequent changes, is all they will accept. Objections to unilateral outside direction include the fact that graduate student thesis research as part of the contract or grant effort could be seriously disrupted, that faculty should not be subject to direction in their research within the university anyway, and that outside direction or control makes the university a servant rather than a coequal with a sponsor. *Mere willingness by the sponsor to pay additional costs is not enough;* there is no fee or profit to compensate for doing what would not be agreed to under a "mutual agreement" provision. This point particularly needs to be emphasized with sponsors who are used to dealing with industry, where imposed changes generally bring an extra fee or profit. At the same time, universities should not expect the right to unilaterally change or exceed the approved scope of work without sponsor agreement.

However, some institutions do accept contract or grant provisions giving the sponsor some degree of direction or control over the research performed. They argue that it is difficult to negotiate the deletion of such provisions, and often the provisions are never implemented. This is a form of Russian roulette, which is sometimes played with many grant and contract provisions.

On balance, a written and implemented policy not to accept outside direction or control is clearly preferable. An institution should, to the maximum extent possible, control its own destiny.

Relation to Educational Programs

Some universities have a policy that any research project undertaken should be closely related to an educational program in a department, school, or college; others do not. More often, it appears to be the major research universities that have no policies insisting on a close relation between research projects and educational programs. The types of projects not so related are often interdisciplinary in nature, without close educational ties to the regular departments of instruction (see chapter 4). The subject matter of such research can ultimately become the knowledge that is taught in perhaps new and emergent departments.

On balance, it seems preferable not to have a policy against research that does not bear a close relationship to the educational program. In some areas, research promising some of the most important advances in knowledge does not relate to present programs of instruction. However, a sound policy could be that research should not *detract* from the educational program. Careful, possibly higher-level review may be desirable in cases where the relation with established departments of instruction is minimal.

Participation of Students

On the surface, a policy regarding participation of students in research may seem almost identical with the previous subject of having a close relation between research and educational programs. However, methods have been developed, as for graduate student research for a thesis or dissertation, whereby interdisciplinary research not closely related to departments of instruction can be accommodated. The participation of students, both undergraduate and graduate, is clearly desirable. However, the advancement of knowledge as a primary university objective does not *have* to be tied to student participation. As a policy or criterion, this could be a *preference,* with more careful review for major projects when it is not fulfilled.

Faculty Supervision

A policy that sponsored research projects must be supervised by a regular member of the faculty is a sensitive one. Many universities insist on it; some have expanded the regular, tenured faculty significantly beyond the number that could be financed were there to be a substantial curtailment of sponsored research funds; some have made "coterminous" faculty appointments whose tenure is keyed to the termination of a sponsored project or projects. Other *types* of professors, associate professors, etc. have been appointed by other institutions. Some universities have developed a ladder of research appointments that do not carry faculty titles, but have most of the same privileges, including the right to supervise projects, that the faculty have (see chapter 5).

It is difficult to see, when all is considered, why there should be any overriding reason for limiting the supervision of research projects to members of the faculty, so long as those who do supervise are professionally qualified and deeply interested. The objective for the advancement of knowledge can be fulfilled, and there should be no detraction from the educational program. Professional titles are not diluted by the appointment of "lower grade" professors, and financial resources are not overcommitted by research-funded faculty appointments.

Qualified and Deeply Interested Personnel

It should hardly need be said that those participating in the research, particularly principal investigators, should be professionally qualified for the research. To a major extent, the qualifications of persons for research should be judged when appointments or promotions are made, including the peer review process discussed in chapter 1. Past performance is also a guide in judging proposals. These attributes may be the primary determinants as to whether a university should endorse a proposal by a civil engineer for a large project to map the moon by astronomical instruments from a balloon, or one by a cosmic-ray physicist to study the environment, or one by an aeronautical engineer to study possible reduction in health hazards from cigarettes. The qualifications of principal investigators show through in the caliber of research proposals in a way no editing can alter significantly.

Because of the tradition of academic freedom in universities, it is particularly important that the persons engaged in research, especially as principal investigators or as co-principal investigators, be deeply interested in the research. Faculty are not often "directed" to do research, they must have a real desire to do it. However, coopting professors—because of their reputations—who do not have a deep interest occurs not infrequently. This may help to "sell" a proposal, but it is damaging in the long run not only to the project but also to the reputation of the institution. On the other hand, there is no reason that persons with outstanding abilities cannot successfully lead more than one or two projects if their interests are really involved.

The qualifications and interest of personnel, particularly of principal investigators, are important criteria for research project endorsement.

Other Policies and Criteria

The availability of buildings, equipment, and services other than those to be paid for directly in a proposal budget should be an obvious criterion for approval of the proposal. However, it sometimes happens that when a grant or contract is received, it is only then discovered that the necessary building space or equipment or services are not available. Careful planning could eliminate many such problems.

University patent and copyright policies are discussed in chapter 6. Those policies should be formulated in such a way as to accommodate sponsored research, and the provisions of sponsored research grants and contracts should be negotiated to comply with those policies.

Many sponsors of research in universities require by statute, regulation, or policy that there be cost-sharing, or even further, matching of costs, in their grants and contracts. Many universities have a sound policy of *promising* cost sharing or matching only to the extent *required*. Awards are rarely affected by cost sharing or matching greater than required and, among other things, promising too much cost sharing can tie up resources that could be used for other purposes. Based on the discussion in the section "For Value Received" in chapter 1, universities are encouraged as a matter of principle to resist terms and conditions requiring cost sharing in grants and contracts.

Publication and Dissemination of Results

Many universities have a policy against the acceptance of research sponsorship that prevents the dissemination and publication of results other than as an exception, and then only under extraordinary conditions. A clear example that has raised furor on many campuses is the performance of research that is classified for reasons of national security. Many institutions as a matter of policy have refused to accept any government contracts in which either the performance of research is classified or there is only access provided to classified information. Some accept contracts that provide access to classified information only on the basis that in some fields of science, and particularly of engineering, there is a necessity to know what is in the classified literature in order to avoid unnecessary and possibly foolish duplication. Still other universities accept classified contracts, often carefully controlled, at least in part on the grounds that academic freedom otherwise would be curtailed for those whose avenues of research interests cannot be pursued outside the barriers of security classification.

Government agencies may control or attempt to control or censor publication and dissemination for other than national security reasons, including patenting. Industrial sponsors may also attempt to obtain the right to control or censor publications for proprietary, "trade secret," or patent purposes. Concerning patents, U.S. patent laws provide that a patent may be obtained on an invention provided that a patent application is filed within one year after publication occurs. On the other hand, many foreign countries forbid patenting if publication occurs even one day before a patent application is filed (under an international convention, filing in the U.S. protects foreign filing for one year). Because foreign patents are important, for the United States government and for industrial sponsors, a delay in publication of four to six months from the date of submission of a proposed publication may be acceptable (actual publication is normally delayed for this period of time, anyway). However, care needs to be taken with regard to student theses and dissertations, since placement in the library constitutes publication. Nevertheless, none of these reasons concerning patents warrants grant or contract provisions providing for censorship or control of dissemination or publication, but only a delay of limited duration.

Other restrictions on publication occur in some unclassified government contracts where a short, innocuous-appearing clause states that results may be published only with approval of the agency. Often aimed at preventing criticism of the agency, such a clause can generally be eliminated on the basis that it violates the Freedom of Information Act. Industrial sponsors may want results withheld from dissemination, but can generally be persuaded to limit the restrictions to proprietary information, furnished by the company, that is clearly marked as such. Both the industrial company and the university benefit from a contract provision to the effect that neither may make reference to the other in any publication, publicity, or advertising without the written consent of the other. A significant amount of research in the social sciences, psychology, and medicine requires confidentiality where human subjects are involved. Publication can be restricted in areas of historical research when the personal papers used as source material have in effect been "classified" by a person's last will and testament.

A policy having as its *objective* the unrestricted publication and dissemination of research results is eminently desirable, but conformance should be moderated by a proviso limiting application to the extent reasonable and practicable.

Conflicts of Interest

The possibility of conflicts of interest in sponsored research has been of concern for a number of years, as evidenced by the December 1964 statement "On Preventing Conflicts of Interest in Government-Sponsored Research at Universities," issued jointly by the American Association of University Professors and the American Council on Education. This statement has been endorsed by many universities and implementing procedures have been adopted; some government contracts contain a clause requiring compliance. The types of potential conflicts of interest that need to be avoided regarding university staff members include:

1. Favoring outside interests, with which the staff member has a financial or consulting relationship, by providing to them preferred treatment as to information, inventions, technical data, purchases, and subcontracts that issue from sponsored research; also, acceptance of gratuities or favors from suppliers or subcontractors, or extension of gratuities or favors to sponsors to obtain grants or contracts.
2. Reduction in the amount of effort that a sponsor had been led to believe would be devoted to a research project, because of conflicting demands on time within the university, or for outside enterprises.
3. Consulting for the government or to government contractors, where objectivity may be questionable because of other interests.

For universities unfamiliar with the AAUP-ACE statement, it should be studied, and endorsement and implementation are recommended. For universities that have not reviewed their policies and practices in this regard for a long time, a refresher would seem in order.

Disclosure of Sponsorship

There have been at some universities instances of research where the true or ultimate sponsorship was hidden and not disclosed at the time a project was initiated. For example, the Central Intelligence Agency may have provided the funds, but the ostensible sponsor was another agency. Then, when the facts were later disclosed, it proved to be embarrassing and damaging to the institution. A clear-cut policy against this type of sponsorship is desirable.

Implementation

As stated at the outset of this chapter, the subjects for a statement of policies and criteria have been discussed, together with the author's conclusions as to the treatment that should be given each one. Whatever is adopted, there is a strong preference for a written statement carefully considered, appropriately endorsed, and widely distributed. Faculty involvement in preparation and approval is important; as a result, implementation will be facilitated.

3

Developing and Implementing Sponsored Research

CONSISTENT WITH THE TITLE OF THIS BOOK, DEVELOPING AND IMPLEmenting sponsored research as described in this chapter do not contain any elements of direction of the research itself. They do include aspects of review, approval, monitoring, and even at some times, control. However, the most important aspect is one of service, a service that facilitates the initiation and performance of research by those who are actually directing and conducting it.

Since World War II, and particularly since about 1960, universities with a significant volume of sponsored research have established central offices to perform at least some of the functions of developing and implementing such research. The responsibilities of these offices vary widely among institutions and their titles are also different. "Research administration" is used as a title in this chapter to cover the functions that seem appropriate for a central office to perform in developing and implementing sponsored research, even though exact titles of offices may range from a dean for graduate affairs and research to an affiliated research foundation. The position of research administration in a university's organizational structure is discussed to only a minor degree in this chapter, when it is important for understanding functions. The subject of organizational structure involving overall management for research is the primary concern of chapter 9.

To a large extent, the functions discussed in this chapter are required only for research sponsored by outside organizations such as government, industry, and private foundations. Only a few functions, such as review and approval, are necessary for research financed from institutional funds.

Development of Proposals

For all practical purposes, proposals can be initiated only by prospective principal investigators, assisted possibly by their associates. However, proposals can be *stimulated* by information concerning prospective sources of funds for research in an area where a proposer has qualifications and interest. The fundamentals of a proposal—what the research is and how it will be performed—should rarely if ever be prepared by anyone other than the person who will perform or lead the research. It has been said that if a professional writer handles the preparation, a proposal loses its integrity and discerning readers can perceive the differences. Editorial assistance, photographs, and particularly assistance with budgets can often be provided by others, resulting in a salutary effect. However, university proposals that are too "slick" or have a "Madison Avenue" complexion can and do backfire. Those responsible for preparing and reviewing research proposals should endeavor to insure a scope of research that is defined broadly enough so that problems with cost disallowances will not be encountered during performance when a change in avenues of exploration becomes desirable (see section below on monitoring).

Proposals for research can sometimes be "tailored" differently to fit the known interests of different sponsors. This can be done without any change at all in the research to be done, and without in any way damaging the validity or integrity of the proposal, by changes in emphasis on relevance, and by implications for potential use or application. The possibilities for such tailoring are much greater for research where the apparent use of research results can be clearly visualized. Also, tailoring requires a fairly complete grasp of the interests of potential sponsors. Research administration can assist in this area but, again, the proposed principal investigator must be intimately involved.

As indicated earlier, budgets are an aspect of proposals in which research administration can provide particular assistance. A fairly comprehensive grasp of the university's accounting system is important to avoid inadequate or wrong advice. A reasonable knowledge of indirect cost principles and their application under various circumstances is necessary (see chapter 7). Promises in a proposal to share the costs, which are required sometimes by law and sometimes by sponsor policies, can become complicated because the amounts actually incurred often require later verification and because situations may change. The total amount of a proposal budget may be influenced by preliminary information regarding the amount probably available from the sponsor.

Review and Approval

The review and approval of proposals within a university generally involve three basic areas of concern: first, intrinsic merit; second, financial aspects; and third, conformance with university policies, which mean many of the policies discussed in chapter 2. These areas of concern, while they can be stated separately, are inevitably interrelated to some degree. For example, a proposal involving a large amount of testing work raises the question as to whether it is research, even though the testing is new and of real interest. A proposal for deep-sea studies requires access to classified information. A proposal involving exploration at remote distances raises a question about the extent to which off-campus indirect cost rates should apply. A sponsor requires 50% cost-sharing in a proposal of high intrinsic merit. These are but a few of the many types of interrelated problems.

Nevertheless, some primary guidance can be provided. With regard to intrinsic merit, the twin principles of academic freedom and research ability, with the latter judged at the time of appointment or promotion, carry a heavy and often overriding weight. As a result, a prospective principal investigator's proposal is often not judged on the basis of intrinsic merit. However, practically all institutions require approval of proposals by the academic department where the research will be conducted, generally by the department head and in some institutions or departments by a research review committee within the department; sometimes these actions do represent judgments of intrinsic merit. Departments can also make judgments on budgets, at least insofar as proposal budgets affect their own financial resources. And if university policies for sponsored research have been soundly formulated and widely distributed, departments can make at least a preliminary determination that these policies have been followed to the extent that they affect research proposals. Interdisciplinary programs can be considered to function as departments if the interdepartmental committees discussed in chapter 4 perform effectively.

Above the departmental level there is an assorted group of paths followed by universities for the review and approval of research proposals, each presumably covering one or more of the three areas of concern. Those in the approval chain can include (in addition to research administration) deans of schools (because school budgets may be affected), business officers (because of effect on finances), deans of graduate schools (because graduate students may be involved), deans of faculty (faculty may be involved), directors of procurement (because of purchases), directors of facilities (facilities may be affected), research boards or committees, provosts, executive vice presidents, and even presidents. In each office there may be more than one person concerned. The complete route is a long and time-consuming chain, and can therefore be costly. To short-circuit the system, an advance one-page summary is sometimes circulated for "sign-off," but this is hardly a careful review.

There are too many points for review and approval of research proposals in some institutions. This can lead to a situation where each person in the chain signs off in the belief that someone else in the chain will catch the problem, but no one in the chain is able to spend enough time or to give enough thought even to see the problem.

The solution is adequate delegation of authority and responsibility to research administration, with proper status for that office in the university hierarchy, as discussed in chapter 9. As far as review and approval of research proposals are concerned, research administration should have the authority for final approval if the responsible department has approved and if the proposal is not for a new project above some fairly high limit (say, $100,000 per year); if it does not conflict with any established university policies; or if research administration does not see some other problem that is not soluble at its level. When research administration is unable to approve a proposal for any one of these reasons, there should be a clear line of authority to someone who can. Of course, when the government mandates certain approvals, as for projects involving human subjects, there must be compliance. Among other things, if research administration does not have the authority discussed above, negotiation with the sponsor of any changes in the proposal as submitted, a frequent occurrence, becomes almost impossible.

Seeking Outside Sponsors

Generally speaking, a potential principal investigator has four sources of information concerning the availability of funds for research from an outside sponsor: (1) the proposer's own knowledge of potential sponsors, (2) colleagues in either the same or another institution, (3) the sponsors themselves, and (4) a university research administration or fund-raising office.

There is little doubt that personal knowledge of sponsor interests and limitations is the best basis on which to prepare and submit a research proposal that will be acted on favorably. Some personal contact with sponsor representatives is valuable, and can be supplemented or often preceded by information from colleagues, from sponsor announcements of various sorts, and from research administration or fund-raising offices. The personal contact may not be possible for smaller proposals, but large proposals clearly warrant it.

It has been noted that, in the major research universities, as compared with those having a smaller research volume, a much *lower* fraction of the research administration function, as it can be formally identified, is devoted to seeking out and developing sources of research support, particularly from federal agencies. In universities having a smaller research volume, as much as half or more of the identified function of research administration is concentrated on this one objective. It has been argued that the major research universities rely on their reputations, but there is some evidence to indicate that, if all other things are equal, some sponsors may lean toward less prestigious institutions.

Most major research universities state that they place primary responsibility for locating sources of research support on their faculty, and for junior faculty they expect the more senior colleagues to help out. Of course, these institutions generally do circulate information concerning promising funding opportunities. It is possible that the faculties of major research universities may have more frequent opportunities to travel and thus to meet with potential sponsor representatives, often through professional society meetings.

In smaller research universities, more funds for faculty travel that lead to personal contacts with sponsors might bring greater dividends than some of the funds spent centrally under the aegis of research administration or fund raising for "sponsor development." If the costs are properly identified, they may be recoverable as costs associated with proposals under the indirect cost element of research administration (see chapter 7).

The vast majority of university research proposals are unsolicited. However, universities do at times receive requests for proposals (RFPs) or requests for quotations (RFQs), often as a result of their requests to be placed on "bidders" lists. Many of these RFPs and RFQs are "wired," in the sense that one or more organizations have already been involved to the extent that they have a distinct advantage in any resulting proposal competition. This, combined with the fact that the resulting research may be very application-oriented, has dissuaded many universities from investing the time and effort necessary to submit a proposal in response to this type of request.

Finally, some believe that political contacts or political pressure can be helpful. Political contacts can on occasion provide information about potential research grants or contracts. There are rumored instances of fairly large university projects being influenced by political pressure. On the other hand, there are rumored instances of political pressure backfiring, so that the use of this kind of persuasion needs to be delicately handled.

Submission of Proposals

It is important that proposals, when formally submitted to a sponsor, carry the signature of a university official having *contractual* authority. In legal terms, a proposal is an offer that, if accepted by the one to whom it is offered, and assuming legal consideration, becomes a binding contract without any further legal technicalities. Since government grants are contracts, according to a ruling of the U.S. Comptroller General, the contractual authority of the official who signs for the university is particularly important for proposals that will result in government grants. There is likely to be no further document, as there is for contracts, where the university's official approval is inscribed. Proposals for private foundation grants may be in a somewhat different situation than proposals for government grants, although use of the same signature authority has advantages.

The person who heads research administration in a university is the logical person to have contractual authority for proposals. Research administration is also the logical channel for actual proposal submission, except where sponsors such as private foundations insist on presidential submission. A single channel is emphasized because of the problems that have been observed where multiple channels have been used. Notwithstanding these observations, there is often much to be gained by potential principal investigators transmitting an *informal* and *unofficial* draft copy of a proposal to a sponsor for comments before a final proposal is prepared. However, principal investigators should be encouraged to seek advice from research administration even at this stage.

Negotiation

Following proposal submission there is often negotiation before consummation of a grant or contract. Of course, preliminary negotiation often takes place with salutary effect before official proposal submission. Negotiation includes three major components: (1) scope of the research, (2) budget, and (3) terms and conditions. Negotiations with regard to scope of research require primarily the participation of the principal investigator. These negotiations on research scope need to be closely coordinated with any changes agreed to in the budget, and research administration can particularly concern itself that there is no implicit or contractual obligation to the performance of research that cannot be accomplished within the funds ultimately provided. At the same time, as mentioned earlier in this chapter with regard to proposals, the scope should be broad enough to encompass changes in the avenues of research exploration.

The terms and conditions of grants and contracts, often called the "boilerplate," cover seemingly endless requirements when the government is the sponsor. Allowable costs, payment, property accounting, patents, copyrights, termination, changes, employment conditions, etc. are only a few of the applicable terms and conditions. Those applicable to government grants are usually contained in a grants manual, which is just as binding contractually as if all the words were in the grant letter of award itself. The requirements of grant manuals are rarely subject to negotiation by a single university, but must generally be approached through some kind of association of universities. Contract terms and conditions may be part of the individual contract or may be contained in a "basic agreement," which is incorporated by reference into each contract between a sponsoring agency and a university. Most of these contract terms and conditions are contained in regulations such as the Armed Services Procurement Regulations (ASPR) issued by the Department of Defense and the Federal Procurement Regulations (FPR) issued by the General Services Administration for civilian agencies. Many contract terms and conditions are negotiable only in the same way as for grant manuals, i.e., through an association of universities, but some, such as a "changes" provision discussed in chapter 2, are negotiable by an individual institution. Using the same analogy as in chapter 2, it is like playing Russian roulette to accept conditions that are contrary to university policies just because they may not be implemented. Some of the policies discussed in chapter 2 become applicable only during negotiation.

Private organizations such as foundations and industry have much greater flexibility than federal agencies, and they are not concerned with many of the conditions affecting government grants and contracts. With foundations, the scope of research and the allowable costs are of primary importance, and for the latter, charges for academic-year faculty salaries and indirect costs generally far outweigh any considerations other than the scope of work. Educating foundations on just these two points could be greatly rewarding. The most important negotiating problems with industry are generally publication and dissemination rights and patent rights.

Then there is the question of legal review during negotiation. Some institutions draw a sharp distinction between grants and contracts insofar as legal review is concerned, but as stated earlier in this chapter, such a distinction does not have much validity for research sponsored by the government. A sound course to follow is to have a highly competent research administration that must seek legal advice only when there has been no legal precedent set for a particular type of grant or contract, term or condition, or in special circumstances such as a project having a very large annual dollar volume.

Acceptance and Activation

All contracts and some grants require acceptance, and that acceptance means a signature by one having contractual authority. Following the same reasoning as for proposals, research administration is the logical place for this authority to reside.

Acceptance normally is the signal for activation of a research project unless, of course, the grant or contract document received is for renewal or continuation. At this point some universities follow a practice of transferring responsibility for the project from research administration to the business office, which thenceforth becomes the primary administrative authority and channel. While this may solve some problems, even greater ones can be created. Written material such as letters, memoranda, and proposals can be transferred, but oral information and conversations rarely can. The administrative relations that research administration has developed with sponsor representatives are often important during project performance and are essential for continuation and renewal; these relations are different from those of the business office, with auditors and disbursing officers. The relations that research administration has or should have with academic departments and principal investigators, having helped in obtaining sponsorship for research, can generally facilitate more willing acceptance when a sponsor requirement must be implemented. Continuing responsibility for sponsored projects within research administration is greatly preferred.

A university account number against which costs can be charged normally activates research project expenditures. Copies of grant or contract instruments should be distributed, including copies of manuals for grants and basic agreements for contracts, to at least the principal investigator and the controller's office. Wider distribution of these multipaged documents, which will rarely if ever be read in their entirety except by research administration and an occasional principal investigator, can be minimized by distributing an administrative digest. Such a digest may include at least the following:

University account number.
Principal investigator.
Department, with location of research.
Sponsor, with sponsor reference number.
Title of research.
Amount of award (plus cumulative if an extension).
Award budget period (plus total period if an extension).
Indirect cost rate.

Two attachments to the administrative digest are recommended, but with a more limited distribution. These are a copy of the approved budget and a summary of all important sponsor requirements for matters such as prior approvals, property accounting, patents, etc., which can be assembled and reproduced in the same form for all or almost all projects from the same sponsor.

The distribution of administrative digests may include:

Principal investigator.
Department head.
Dean of school.
Dean of faculty.
Dean of graduate school.
Controller.
Purchasing.
Personnel.
Development office.
Public relations.

Monitoring

Little monitoring of the performance of sponsored research goes on in any university. To insure performance, reliance is placed almost entirely on the judgment of principal investigators. However, there have been disallowances of costs by government agencies when research strayed significantly and evidently from the approved scope, as in the case of a project calling for a laboratory investigation, which a principal investigator decided to supplement by a field trip. Proposing and negotiating as broad a scope as possible can minimize but certainly not eliminate the problem. A general reminder to principal investigators may also help.

A somewhat different but related problem of much greater cost disallowances has been encountered in recent years. This is the matter of "late cost transfers," which are transfers of cost, at some time after the cost was incurred, to a government project from some other account such as another government project or a university activity. Such cost transfers can sometimes be justified, but the justification must be well documented. Research administration should be best qualified to approve or reject requests for late cost transfers because of its greater knowledge of research scope and its relations with sponsor representatives who can approve, if such approval is necessary.

While there may be little monitoring of research performance in universities, there is intensive monitoring of research expenditures in some universities. In its most complete version, this takes the form of a central preaudit and control over *all* research project commitments before they can even become an expenditure. Cost overruns are a problem, particularly for some universities. But overly tight control over expenditures removes so much authority from a principal investigator that there is inevitably a concomitant and human loss in sense of responsibility. Under almost *any* system *some* cost overruns are inevitable, and too much pressure to stay within project budgets can lead to unjustified cost transfers to other projects, or to other improprieties. A budget supplement or some other financial device is essential to cover such overruns; this might come from the *ostensible* use of indirect cost reimbursements, discussed in chapter 7, or from funds otherwise available internally for research. Probably the best method of minimizing cost overruns without much paper shuffling is for research administration to plot trend lines on project expenditures each month, and to take appropriate action when these trend lines forecast financial troubles.

Implementing Sponsor Requirements

As stated earlier, sponsor requirements in both grants and contracts for research, particularly from the government, cover a wide gamut indeed. They can range from an animal keeper's compliance with animal care manuals to a president's implementation of affirmative action plans. Many if not most sponsor requirements are outside the scope of research administration authority in any university. Research administration does, however, have a responsibility to bring these requirements to the attention of other university offices that have the authority for implementation. Some of the other chapters in this book, particularly chapter 8, cover some of these obligations.

There are some kinds of sponsor requirements for which a mechanism can and should be implemented within research administration. One of these involves prior approvals, where the sponsor requires certain kinds of commitments or expenditures to be approved centrally in the university or where the approval of the sponsor itself is required. The kinds of items for which such approvals are necessary may include foreign travel, purchase orders or subcontracts of a particular variety, overtime payments, changes in scope of research, and changes in certain budget categories. In some institutions responsibility for the prior approvals that must be obtained from a sponsor is left with principal investigators, but a preferred procedure and one often insisted on by sponsors is for these prior approvals to be initiated by principal investigators, with routing through and endorsement by research administration.

Progress reports at least annually, with final reports on research performed, are prescribed in practically all sponsored research grants and contracts. If not prescribed, as in grants from private foundations, some sort of report or publication is important for the maintenance of good sponsor relationships. While the preparation of such reports and publications is clearly a responsibility of principal investigators, many of the most effective research administrations monitor and follow up on report submission.

In practically all government contracts of the cost type, equipment purchased with government funds or furnished by the government must be recorded, inventoried periodically, and accounted for. Some grants contain similar requirements, as in the case of a sponsor that may specify transfer of equipment to another university if the principal investigator transfers. When a university has a property accounting system for all equipment acquired, no matter what the source of funds, a requirement to account for sponsor property should be easily accommodated; unfortunately, many shortcomings have been observed. In other institutions, research administration is generally a good location for sponsor-mandated property accounting since, among other things, costs can be recovered as part of the research administration element of indirect costs.

Inventions and patents are discussed in some detail in chapter 6. Most sponsored research, except for some private foundation grants, contains requirements pertaining to inventions and patents; generally speaking, annual and final invention reports are required. Unless there is a separate office within a university to handle inventions and patents, research administration should have the responsibility for obtaining these reports and transmitting them to sponsors.

Other special or selective sponsor requirements can in general also be handled best by research administration.

Completion and Termination

In the same sense that sponsored research projects require a reasonably regular system for initiation, so, too, there need to be provisions for completion or termination. Completion is not necessarily intended to mean full completion of the research itself, but an anticipated and recognized date beyond which no research may be performed and no costs incurred except certain recognized completion costs such as might apply to inventions, property dispositions, etc. Commitments that do not become costs before completion are rarely honored.

Termination is different. It involves a notice from the sponsor terminating research *before* the agreed-on completion date. In grants there is often a provision for consultation between the sponsor and the grantee before a termination notice is issued. In contracts the same process may occur, but is not provided for contractually. In the event of termination there are generally provisions for the reimbursement of all costs incurred up to the date of termination, costs beyond that date necessary to comply with contract or grant requirements, and the costs for liquidating commitments that cannot reasonably be canceled. Many universities, perhaps for the reason that terminations are so rare, have not made adequate provisions in their personnel policies for terminal leave pay, in which case such pay is not allowable as a project termination cost. For large laboratories, the government has on rare occasion furnished an amount that can be set aside as a termination reserve to help soften the financial impact of a termination action.

Research Administration Organization

Research administration in some universities is organized internally so that persons specialize in one or more external sponsors. This may be reasonable if the large majority of research administration effort is devoted to seeking outside sources of support. If a more balanced and complete research administration (as discussed in this chapter) is the objective, then rapport with academic departments and principal investigators becomes of major importance, and research administration may be better oriented to institutional departments, each person having researchers in several departments or interdisciplinary programs as his or her "clients." In addition, and funds permitting, at least one person almost exclusively concerned with outside sources of funds, and possibly legislative matters as well, can be valuable.

Research administration is still, after all, administration, and administration tends to be suspect in varying degrees by faculty members. Receptivity and understanding can lead to ready acceptance. An allocation that research administration can use to fill researchers' needs, which cannot be charged to projects or departmental funds, is worth more than it costs. Personal visits to laboratories and academic offices help to counteract the belief that administrators are not interested in the research. In the last analysis, research administration is more than a paperwork business; it is a people business, too.

4

Interdisciplinary Research

THE OUTSTANDING CAPABILITY OF UNIVERSITIES TO PERFORM RESEARCH by exploring, defining, and explaining phenomena in various disciplines has long been universally acknowledged. However, dealing with the interactions of people, things, and the laws of nature almost inevitably requires the use and knowledge of more than one discipline. Although this kind of process or synthesis has taken place ever since man began ascending the ladder of knowledge, it is now dignified with the name of an "interdisciplinary" enterprise. If the advancement of knowledge that is not peculiar to any one discipline is involved, then it can properly be called interdisciplinary research. In recent years government expenditures in particular have been increased substantially for the support of interdisciplinary research in areas that have a bearing on energy, housing, environment, transportation, and many more objectives that are broader than the traditional disciplines of science.

Some have asserted that universities, or at least many universities, do not have the orientation or flexibility to perform interdisciplinary research successfully, that since they are discipline-oriented and traditional by nature, they do not provide the right climate or organizational environment for interdisciplinary scholars, and that the scholars from different disciplines have little motivation to work together toward common goals. Some of these assertions have proved to be true at some universities. In fact, it has been said that where interdisciplinary research has been successfully conducted at universities, it is in spite of rather than because of the university management and climate provided. Therefore, it is a challenge to management for research to help solve the problems that are in many ways peculiar to universities for the performance of interdisciplinary research and to provide the organizational structure and motivating factors that will make it flourish.

Little is devoted in this chapter to the internal organization, goal setting, types of specialization, and other elements affecting the performance of interdisciplinary research; several studies have examined these problems and their results are worth examination. Rather, what are discussed here are largely those aspects of management within the university structure as a whole that have a bearing on the initiation, organization, and operation of interdisciplinary projects.

Interdisciplinary versus Multidisciplinary Research

It is necessary to distinguish between interdisciplinary research and multidisciplinary research, as these terms have sometimes been used synonymously. As the term is used in this volume, interdisciplinary research involves use of the skills, techniques, and knowledge of two or more disciplines toward a common goal or goals. In the course of its performance it generally requires frequent interchanges of ideas and results among practitioners of different disciplines, with the ideas and results of one stimulating or reinforcing the research of others. A common goal (or goals) is probably the most important characteristic, whether it be an immediately relevant goal for the solution of an environmental problem or a more long-range goal of understanding phenomena whose utility or application are not particularly apparent.

Multidisciplinary research, on the other hand, may involve the same number and types of fields as interdisciplinary research, but the common goals and the interchanges are largely absent. An example of the mechanics of multidisciplinary research would be the melding together of proposals, each without much adjustment, for specific research topics in physics, chemistry, and mathematics, then submitting the combined proposals, possibly under a single title and introduction, and, after award of a grant or contract, distributing the funds in about the same amounts as in the original melded proposals. There is no intention here of denigrating multidisciplinary research. It has its place in a university environment, and it can be much more easily accommodated than interdisciplinary research, since the components can be carried out within the traditional departmental structures, with only the addition of some sort of administrative coupling, but little else in common. There may sometimes be funding advantages, compared with separate proposal submissions, since one or more strong proposals may carry along one that is not so strong.

However, multidisciplinary research is not interdisciplinary research; it does not have the common goals and the frequent interchange of ideas and results.

Teaching versus Research

In chapter 2 there was discussion of a research policy or criterion that research should be closely related to the educational program. In other words, such a policy or criterion should state that research must be related to and in some way be tied in with teaching. But what to teach? In a field of interdisciplinary activity that is relatively new, research and scholarly activity must *precede* teaching, since knowledge in the interdisciplinary field needs to be acquired before it can be taught. Black studies, which have had problems in some universities, may have been seriously hampered by the lack of *new* knowledge to be taught. In some cases, what is learned evolves naturally into a new discipline, and many examples could be given, dating back many years. More recently, biochemistry, biophysics, business administration, international studies, etc. have flowered into departments or schools, where the beginnings were as interdisciplinary endeavors. In fact, except for mathematics, are there any disciplines that are "pure" in the sense that they do not include parts of what are or were other disciplines?

The conclusion is as it was in chapter 2: interdisciplinary research could be seriously curtailed if there is insistence on a close relation between teaching and research.

Basic versus Applied Research

In interdisciplinary research the use to which new knowledge will be put is often more apparent than for research in more traditional disciplines, particularly the natural sciences; however, the key word is "often," not "always." Problem solving of the type sometimes called interdisciplinary research can be primarily the application of knowledge, with little research toward the advancement of knowledge. In this case, it probably has little place in a university under the rubric of research, although other considerations such as furtherance of the public interest and public welfare may fully justify its existence.

On the other hand, other interdisciplinary research with an apparent end use has been carried on, and appropriately so, in universities, despite the fact that it may be disparaged with the appellation of applied research. As discussed in chapter 1, what is important is the extent to which a project is devoted to the advancement of knowledge, not whether there is potential utility for that knowledge. For 25 years interdisciplinary research in plasma physics has been going on, with the ultimate goal of attaining fusion power through the thermonuclear reaction, which may still be 25 years away. The growth in emphasis on advances in knowledge is clearly evident from the fact that the plasma physics section of the American Physical Society has grown since its inception in 1959 to be one of the largest sections.

Motivation and Team Effort

Two of the most difficult problems encountered in interdisciplinary research in universities are the motivation of faculty members who participate, or whose participation is desired, and the adjustment of those faculty members to a team effort, in which each member's research depends to some degree on the work and research results of someone else.

With regard to motivation, faculty members are discipline-oriented and their careers depend largely on the judgment accorded them by their departmental colleagues. As has been said before in this volume, faculty members are often accustomed to acting like independent entrepreneurs with regard to their research. As an additional problem, faculty members' willingness to participate in an interdisciplinary program will be seriously curtailed unless the achievements in that program are recognized for promotions and advancements. In chapter 1 there was discussion of outside peer evaluation to help in decisions on promotions and advancements, and these are probably even more important for interdisciplinary programs than they are for more regular departmental positions. A steering committee, composed of faculty members from cooperating departments, as discussed later in this chapter, can be helpful in a feedback process to the departments about research performance and capabilities of faculty participants. There is a radical solution, which is to permit faculty promotions and advancements to be acted on without confirmation by a home department.

One important aspect of motivation is the willingness of departments to cooperate in providing released time for members of their faculty to participate in interdisciplinary projects. Practices vary, but in general, departments are loath to cooperate if they do not receive compensation for time released for participation in an interdisciplinary project. Sometimes they must request compensation from their dean or even higher authority, which may be justified in some cases but not in others. Compensation generally takes the form of retention in the departmental budget of the funds released by charging a faculty member's time to an interdisciplinary project.

Conquering the unwillingness of persons, which can even be an inability, to participate in a team effort is not an easy task. Sometimes this reluctance can be endured by parceling out some quite separable and independent piece of research; at other times, conquering the unwillingness is not worth the effort. It is in this area that the project director's powers of persuasion and ability to handle people become of great importance.

In some cases a short-term ad hoc interdisciplinary project can attract members of the faculty from participating departments because it is not of sufficient duration to interrupt their careers. On the other hand, a long-term program can hold out the prospect of a new and rewarding career. Medium-length projects with an end point can be the most difficult from the standpoint of attracting staff. Senior faculty who have already "made their marks" can be much more willing to enter an interdisciplinary project than more junior colleagues who have not yet established themselves.

Extra compensation has occasionally been used as a motivating force. Government cost principles forbid such extra compensation for project work unless it is approved by the sponsoring agency. A faculty member's base salary can, however, be increased without sponsor approval so long as teaching or other nonproject activities pay for time or effort at the higher rate.

Project Director

For the project director of an interdisciplinary project, particularly a large project, the most important qualification is not necessarily that of being an outstanding scientist or engineer, although this is highly desirable if it is combined with the other qualifications needed. One might say that the qualifications needed are more like those required of a university provost or president, and some presidents were in fact project directors of interdisciplinary projects at an earlier time. Of course, a working knowledge *is* required of the scientific or professional fields covered by the project.

But the qualifications needed most are *leadership, administrative ability,* and *power of persuasion*. These are clearly not as necessary for a small project as a large one, for which professional research qualifications then become of major importance.

Should the project director be a regular member of the faculty? In the great majority of instances encountered, this has been so, but not always. There are several reasons why he or she should be a regular faculty member, the most important probably being status within the university community; how important that status is depends on the institution. There is no *implicit* reason why a project director must be a regular member of the faculty. Other *kinds* of faculty appointments are being made to avoid the problems associated with regular faculty status. And full-time nonfaculty positions are growing, as discussed later in this chapter and in more detail in chapter 5.

University Organization for Interdisciplinary Research

Several different locations for interdisciplinary research programs within university organizational structures have been encountered. Sometimes they have been attached to departments, but more often to schools or colleges.

There may be administrative conveniences in such arrangements, but if faculty members or graduate students or others participate, whose regular affiliation is with another department or school, there is generally unhappiness. More often and more logically, interdisciplinary projects that cross departmental and school lines are the responsibility of a provost, or better, a vice-president for research or some other institutional officer who has at least the rank of a dean in the university hierarchy. In this way, interdisciplinary projects have a status somewhat similar to departments, but without teaching responsibility.

How then are the usual departmental type of responsibilities that are handled by discipline-oriented projects fulfilled in the case of interdisciplinary projects? Quite often, steering committees are appointed, composed of senior faculty members, often department chairmen, from departments involved in the research in one way or another. The more effective such committees are, the more the university can be assured that its policies and criteria for research are being fulfilled. A most important role is "carrying the word" to departments about the effectiveness of faculty members who participate in an interdisciplinary project, so that they will not lose their motivation, but will be recognized for promotions and advancements when warranted.

Interdisciplinary projects are sometimes organized into research institutes, either a single institute for each project or program, or one institute embracing a number of projects or programs, each with different sorts of goals. The latter, where it has been observed, has led to a superstructure and climate that is somewhat alien to the mainstream of the university itself. Institutes generally connote a considerably larger organization than an interdisciplinary project per se. At some point, perhaps between $500,000 and $1,000,000 a year, a careful review should be made to ascertain probable future growth and lines of growth and to establish guidelines. Periodic reviews thereafter are desirable.

Personnel

The problems of motivation and team effort of participating faculty members have already been discussed, and although some suggestions have been made, there are no complete answers.

Full-time research appointments of professional personnel who are not *regular* members of the faculty are almost always needed for an interdisciplinary project of any magnitude. The status of such personnel is discussed in chapter 5. If the program is established within a proper organizational framework, it should have the same authority as a regular department or school with regard to appointments. Just because an interdisciplinary project needs someone with a physics background does not mean that the appointment requires review and approval by the physics department.

Graduate student participation in most interdisciplinary projects insofar as thesis research is concerned is apt to be lighter than for single-discipline projects; no definitive statistics seem to be available. Contributing to the problem are the facts that interdisciplinary research is more mission oriented; that it involves team effort, which is difficult to reconcile with the requirements of a graduate thesis; that a faculty supervisor may not be easily found; and that the interdisciplinary research itself is not a recognized field of study. The fact that some graduate students do participate and produce acceptable theses from interdisciplinary research is perhaps a tribute to ingenuity.

Initiation and University Funding

An interdisciplinary research program cannot be launched full-blown on a large and amorphous basis; it needs to concentrate on one or more specific and reasonably small-scale undertakings. There are too many examples of grandiose plans that led to failure. Success in smaller or fewer endeavors will breed confidence, earn financial support, attract persons of high caliber and, in the natural course of events, lead to broader and more comprehensive enterprises.

In order to initiate a successful interdisciplinary project, it is essential that there be a core of university funding. Part of the core can be made up of contributed time, but some requirements for hard cash inevitably occur. Even when such funds have been available in significant amounts, there have been instances in which interdisciplinary projects did not succeed, probably because of failures in other respects. However, the author knows of no examples where such projects succeeded without a financial commitment of some size from the institution.

An interdisciplinary program, as it continues with time, often embraces two or more separately funded projects. If the program consists of two or more projects, it should have a regular university allocation to cover the sort of expenses that are included in the departmental administration element of indirect costs, as discussed in chapter 7. This allocation can be recouped through the indirect cost reimbursement. If such an allocation is not provided, proper sorting out of such things as office supplies, telephones, etc. as direct costs to each of the projects involved becomes complicated. Furthermore, a separate and lower indirect cost rate must be negotiated for the program, since one element, departmental administration costs, is absent. If the program consists of one contract or grant, it can pay for all departmental types of costs as direct costs, but again, if this is done, a separate and lower indirect cost rate must be negotiated.

Facilities and Identity

Multidisciplinary projects can generally operate successfully with each discipline housed in its normal facility, but this just does not work for an interdisciplinary project. If the common goals, frequent interchanges of ideas and results, and team effort necessary are to be realized, a common facility is essential so that persons from different disciplines can work together and "rub shoulders." It is possible that the greater success achieved by interdisciplinary programs involving mostly theoretical research such as in the social sciences is due to the fact that experimental research requires much more expensive facilities. Some critics have claimed that large interdisciplinary projects with their own facilities become aloof from the mainstream of university activity; perhaps some of this is inevitable. Wise management for research, which takes into consideration the welfare of the university as a whole, can help to minimize the problem.

A successful interdisciplinary project needs not only a separate facility, but also both an identity and an organization separate from the usual departmental structure. The larger the project, the more sophisticated the organization must be. Symposia, colloquia, and publications in the interdisciplinary field are desirable to give it visibility.

The aspects mentioned above are particularly important for long-term interdisciplinary endeavors. In ad hoc or short-term projects many short cuts are possible.

Sponsor Attitudes

In the preceding discussion, internal problems of universities in undertaking interdisciplinary research were analyzed. Sponsors, whether government agencies or private organizations, need to recognize these problems and to help with their solutions. In particular, there should be no expectation that rapid launching of a large effort will be successful; universities do not shuffle people around rapidly, no matter what the impetus.

Whereas the costs involved in preparing and submitting modest proposals can usually be paid for by the normal indirect costs associated with university research activities, the costs of larger-scale enterprises cannot. In line with the concept that a large program cannot be launched full-blown, a feasibility or study type of grant or contract, lasting perhaps a year or more, can generally lay the soundest foundation for building an interdisciplinary research structure.

Sharing with sponsors the costs of sponsored projects is a requirement that is undermining the financial integrity of many institutions. Cost sharing in interdisciplinary projects is particularly objectionable; participating departments resent having "their" funds used for this purpose, and also resent the use of general university funds that might otherwise have gone to them. Instead of cost sharing, it seems reasonable that an "institutional allowance" should be provided *over and above costs*. This institutional allowance could be used to pay back the institution's original contribution to the program, to provide an incentive for departments to participate in the program, and to furnish the wherewithal for modest research efforts not within the scope of work of the contract or grant.

The larger the interdisciplinary program becomes, the more necessary it is to have a long-term commitment by the sponsor. Personnel commitments for substantial periods of time and the need to amortize buildings and equipment paid for by institutional funds are obvious. Less obvious, but not less important, are the tone and flavor inherent in a recognizably stable organization. Neither the institution itself nor the participating departments can be expected to provide the stability needed without sponsor assurances.

Finally, for reasons that are not clear, some sponsors that are concerned with interdisciplinary research do not seem to recognize the need for liberal terms and conditions in grants and contracts. More sympathetic treatment is necessary if for no other reasons than that interdisciplinary projects and programs are more difficult to organize and operate than ordinary ones, and qualified faculty are more difficult to attract and hold. Thus, liberal terms and conditions in grants and contracts can help.

5

Professional Personnel Other than Faculty

AN ADEQUATE AND RECOGNIZED STATUS FOR NONFACULTY PROFESSIONAL personnel engaged in research is neglected in many universities. Part of the reason undoubtedly is that this sort of position has existed in universities in any significant numbers for only about half the lifetime of persons in this category who are approaching retirement age, whereas faculty ranks can probably be said to have been created when the oldest universities emerged from infancy.

Nationwide statistics on nonfaculty professional personnel are far from complete. The National Science Foundation reports that, as of fall 1975, there were in the U.S. 17,000 full-time postdoctorals having no academic rank, who were appointed by graduate science departments; presumably all of these were involved in research in one way or another.* It is likely that this figure does not include a number of doctorals appointed to interdisciplinary programs outside of academic department channels. It clearly does not include professional personnel who do not have the doctoral degree, but who are employed for research programs. No national figures are available on these persons having only a bachelor's or master's degree, but if experience at Princeton University can be extrapolated, the numbers are at least equal to or greater than the numbers of doctorals. Based on these figures, there are across the country a large number of nonfaculty professionals engaged in research in universities. Their status thus becomes a matter of concern to sound management for research.

The policies and procedures universities use for the appointment and employment of nonfaculty professionals vary over wide limits. When such persons are needed, some institutions seemingly seek solutions by making additional regular faculty appointments (although these are sometimes called "research professors") without adequate consideration of the long-term implications or financial obligations; this practice may have contributed to the saturation of tenured faculty ranks at many institutions. Some universities have created a different category of professor, whose tenure is limited to the duration of a project and who may or may not have

---

* "Science Resources Studies Highlights," NSF 76-320 (Washington, D.C.: National Science Foundation, 1976).

43

faculty voting rights, teaching opportunities, or other perquisites. Some state universities may employ these persons under civil service; affiliated research foundations may be the employer in other cases. It is unlikely that these types of appointments are included in the NSF figure stated above for postdoctorals, thus increasing even further the numbers of professionals engaged in research who are not fully fledged faculty members.

In quite a few universities the title "research associate" is used for nonfaculty professional personnel, but without any clear definition of status, perquisites, and other personnel matters, and some research associates may have held that rank for as much as twenty years. Other titles are used elsewhere, in varying degrees. At some institutions the appointment, advancement, titles, etc. of nonfaculty professional personnel may be almost entirely a departmental or school prerogative, which can lead to personnel problems and even to sponsor questioning of consistency in employment practices and compensation policies.

If nonfaculty professional personnel are as important to research in universities as the evidence seems to indicate, there is much to be gained, which will lead to improvements in research performance, if there are well-considered and well-implemented policies and procedures for titles and ranks, terms of employment, perquisites, benefits, etc. Among other things, grievances, equal employment, and similar personnel actions can be facilitated; second-class status can be minimized.

It is possible to distinguish between two different purposes for which nonfaculty professionals are employed for research projects and programs in universities. The first purpose is for the advancement of knowledge, and in the remainder of this chapter, persons employed for this purpose are referred to as the research staff. The second purpose is for the professional support of research in ways that will make it possible for those who advance knowledge to perform their research or to perform it more effectively; persons employed for this purpose are referred to in this book as the professional support staff. It is clear that the dividing line between these two categories of research staff and professional support staff may be rather vague for some projects, but the *primary* purpose for which a person is employed can be used as the determinant. In addition, persons can switch from one category to the other if they have the qualifications and if there is a need, although experience indicates that such switching is rare.

Research Staff

The research staff, as defined here, consists of those nonfaculty professionals who have as their primary function the performance of research;

they may even lead research, and are expected to have publishable research results. The potentiality of using research staff for supervision of research projects was discussed in chapter 2, and the importance of having such persons for interdisciplinary projects was discussed in chapter 4. Other (discipline-oriented) projects or programs of substantial size cannot be staffed adequately just with regular members of the faculty, graduate students, and nonprofessionals.

Titles and ranks fill a human need for recognition that is sometimes too little appreciated. Unstructured appointments to a "project research staff" or as a research associate if the same title applies whether someone is one or twenty years past the Ph.D. are not uncommon, but some prestige is missing. For universities that have devoted considerable time and effort to examining the subject, ranks and titles for the research staff have evolved that parallel to some degree the ranks accorded to the faculty. This has the significant advantage that qualifications, *insofar as research is concerned,* can be measured against similar qualifications for faculty. However, there may be subtle considerations for avoiding full parallelism in titles. Titles in which the discipline appears have advantages. A four-rank structure might then become: senior research physicist (equivalent to full professor), research physicist, associate research physicist, assistant research physicist. The word "research" may be deleted in each case, although this word provides a tie with the category title of research staff. Other titles can obviously be used.

The title of research associate has existed for many years, primarily applying to a postdoctoral appointment of limited duration. It can be retained for this purpose if its distinguishing characteristic continues to be one of *limited duration,* to avoid confusion with appointees in a ladder of appointments, who are expected to be employed over a relatively long period.

Professional Support Staff

Professional support staff members, as defined here, have as a primary purpose the support of research in ways that will make it possible for those who advance knowledge to perform their research or to perform it more effectively. The kinds of trained professionals needed for this purpose in university research include engineers of all types, computer specialists, chemical analysts, statisticians, and many more. Large experimental projects in particular require engineers for the design, fabrication, maintenance, operation, and improvement of complex apparatus and instrumentation. The computer specialist is penetrating all aspects of the university;

the others are increasingly needed as it becomes more difficult to put additional rungs of knowledge on the ladder for the ascent of man.

Most persons who fall into the professional support staff category have terminated their formal education at either a bachelor's or master's degree, although there are some with the Ph.D. There are no national statistics that would be applicable at all. At Princeton University the ratio of professional support staff (as defined earlier) to research staff is slightly more than 1:2 for the usual type of discipline-oriented university research projects, although individual projects have much different ratios. At Princeton's large Plasma Physics Laboratory, however, which is heavily oriented to experimental research, the professional support staff is more than one and one-half times the research staff.

Titles and ranks for the professional support staff are more difficult to establish than for the research staff, in the sense that no parallelism with the faculty is possible insofar as qualifications are concerned, and similar criteria or means for judging appointments and advancements are difficult, if not impossible. Two ranks have been used, of which one is senior professional support staff member. Another group of titles and ranks includes engineer, engineering associate, engineering assistant, etc. Administrative titles such as group leader, section head, etc. are at best only a partial solution. However, as stated with regard to the research staff, the human need for recognition in terms of a rank and title is still present.

Appointments, Promotions, and Changes in Salary

In some institutions the academic departments or interdisciplinary projects have the authority, or most of the authority, to appoint, promote, or change salary for nonfaculty professional personnel. In other instances, recommendations are forwarded to personnel offices. In some cases, recommendations may be handled in a manner similar to that used for comparable members of the faculty.

If a university desires a climate in which research will flourish, and if it desires to promote the performance of that research, there is every reason to apply the same high standards for research qualifications to the research staff as are applied to the faculty. One can argue for even more rigorous standards, since research is generally their only function, whereas faculty have the teaching function also. Applying these standards means, for the more senior ranks of research staff at least, using the outside peer evaluation procedure as well as internal review, as was discussed in chapter 1 for the faculty. A dean of faculty or other officer with ultimate or de facto authority for faculty appointments is more apt to be attuned to the characteristics of research personalities than is a personnel office that usually handles machinists, electricians, typists, etc. An advisory committee composed of senior faculty and research staff personnel is a valuable adjunct in reviewing recommended senior appointments and advancements. Handling research staff appointments, promotions, and salary scales in ways comparable to those used for the faculty also helps to minimize second-class citizenship. One might even dream that some regularization of these positions throughout the country would someday come to pass, with salutary effects.

For the professional support staff the problems are different. Creative design and engineering-type qualifications of a high level are often required, but original research abilities are not. Sometimes professional support staff appointments are handled through the same channels as research staff (without outside peer evaluations); sometimes they can be handled reasonably well through a personnel office that has been properly staffed for this purpose.

Term of Appointment

To avoid financial obligation of the sort that would be involved in awarding tenure to nonfaculty professionals whose salaries are almost always paid from sponsored research funds, or "soft money," other schemes need to be developed. One solution, most applicable to senior ranks, is to provide tenure with a small "t," which means that appointment continues so long as the work performed is satisfactory and research in the university continues to be of a type and scope requiring the appointee's professional skills. For less senior ranks, annual appointments appear more suitable, and for some ranks, such as a postdoctoral research associate, it is probably wise to specify a limit on the number of reappointments (two is often used) in order to avoid any implicit or moral obligation for continuation, i.e., up or out.

In addition to the above aspects, consideration should be given to the fact that sponsored projects close out and they can sometimes be terminated at all sorts of times during a year (see chapter 3). Thus, provisions need to be made for termination notices and/or terminal leave pay, except in those few cases in which the terminal date of an appointment and that of a project coincide. Dismissal for cause, which may involve appropriate grievance procedures, does not typically warrant termination notices or terminal leave pay.

A termination notice, specifying severance after a certain period of time has elapsed, has the distinct disadvantage that a recipient is apt to spend the remaining period in job seeking, with little attention to work. Terminal leave pay, also called severance pay, is therefore often preferred. Both procedures, however, have their places.

The amount of time covered by termination notices or terminal leave pay can range from one month to as much as one year, depending on rank and length of service. Both are allowable under government projects if they are specified in formal personnel policies. Large-scale terminations involved in concluding a major project are generally treated as a direct charge to the project. Smaller-scale or individual termination payments are best treated as part of a personnel benefit pool chargeable along with pensions, social security, unemployment insurance, etc. prorated to all salaries.

Outside Consulting

Outside consulting has been permitted for the faculty primarily for three fundamental reasons. First, research horizons can be broadened and research capabilities can be improved from outside relationships. Second, particularly in more applied areas like engineering, the faculty member is expected to benefit as a teacher from association with that segment of business or government that might ultimately be expected to employ his or her students. Third, at least to many of those who engage in it, outside consulting is sanctioned because of the opportunity to earn additional income.

Some universities that permit faculty to engage in outside consulting deny this privilege to nonfaculty professionals, while other universities permit it. In other words, they are sometimes treated as industrial employees, who rarely have the chance to consult. With regard to the reasons for permitting or encouraging consulting by the faculty, the second reason listed in the previous paragraph does not apply to nonfaculty personnel except in the rare instances when they do teach. The first and third reasons are valid, at least for the research staff. On balance, outside consulting under carefully controlled conditions appears warranted.

Among the standards that should be applied to outside consulting by nonfaculty professionals, some of the most important are contained in the section "Conflicts of Interest" in chapter 2 and in the AAUP-ACE statement referenced in that section. Frequency of consulting should be set and an annual report of consulting actually performed has sometimes been required. No outside organizations should be permitted through a consulting relationship to obtain a preferred position as a result of the consultant's employment by the university or based on information emanating from university research. It is important that consulting agreements should not obligate the individuals with regard to inventions, copyrightable material, and data in any way that conflicts with university policies or sponsor requirements.

Nonfaculty Professionals as Teachers

There are some nonfaculty professionals who want to teach and are qualified to teach. They may be wanted for teaching, but not for enough time, or not on a regular enough basis, to make them members of the faculty; or there may be no faculty positions open. Some universities find a way to use such persons in teaching; some do not, or may not want to.

Where they do teach, they often have no change in their regular research titles. Sometimes the designation "and lecturer" is added after the research title. On occasion they are given assimilated faculty titles, such as "with rank of associate professor." Practices vary as to whether these titles carry with them faculty voting privileges. Such titles clearly should not carry tenure with them, so that periodic (such as annual) renewal of teaching status is the general practice.

Any reasons against using nonfaculty professionals as teachers, if they are qualified and needed, seem shortsighted.

Salary Scales

Salaries for personnel in the research staff ranks should be reasonably comparable to those in the faculty ranks for the same discipline *if* qualifications, benefits, and perquisites are reasonably comparable. However, the absence of complete tenure and the lack of a "professor" title may necessitate some differential if the best researchers are wanted or needed. The opportunity to lead research projects as principal investigators, as discussed in chapter 2, clearly makes a university more attractive for this type of position.

The professional support staff members have jobs more closely identifiable with positions in industry than with those traditionally associated with university research. Salary scales nearer to those in industry may therefore be necessary to attract highly qualified personnel. If outside consulting is not permitted for the professional support staff, then the situation is even more like that in industry.

Benefits and Service Arrangements

If the objective of minimizing second-class citizenship is accepted, then the benefits and service arrangements for nonfaculty professionals should closely approximate those for faculty. A manual periodically revised and setting forth the benefits and service arrangements along with other conditions of employment is important. Of all the items that could be cited, only a few are mentioned below.

Leaves of absence with pay (or sabbatical leaves) are valuable to the person, and the cost of such leaves, along with other benefit costs, can be recovered through a fringe benefit rate charged to sponsored research salaries. Grievance procedures in the event of termination for cause are not really a benefit, but they do require careful coverage in a personnel manual. Athletic facilities and events and opportunities for study are sometimes forgotten. Other sorts of benefits may be overlooked because they do not appear in benefit manuals, such as a university league originally founded for the spouses of faculty members and administrators, but which are now also open to spouses of members of the research staff and professional support staff.

6

Patents and Copyrights

PATENTS AND COPYRIGHTS ARE BOTH PROVIDED FOR IN THE SAME sentence of the United States Constitution. Section 8 of the Constitution states that "The Congress shall have power . . . to promote the progress of science and useful arts, by securing for limited times to authors and inventors the exclusive right to their respective writings and discoveries[.]" Collectively, patentable inventions and copyrightable materials are sometimes referred to as "intellectual property" and patents and copyrights as "intellectual property rights."

Intellectual property is one of the primary outputs of research and other research-like scholarly endeavors. Some would call it *the* primary output, but new knowledge in the form of theories, discoveries of laws of nature or scientific principles, etc. is not patentable, although descriptions in the format in which such knowledge is presented are copyrightable. Patents and copyrights have some similarities in the senses discussed above, but in most other respects they are dissimilar and should be treated separately.

Patents

A patent is a grant to an inventor by the government of the right to exclude others for a limited time from making, using, or selling his or her invention in the country where the patent is granted. The word "discoveries" in the Constitution is almost always taken to mean "inventions" in terms of patent law. An invention, to be patentable, must by law represent a *new* and *useful* art, machine, manufacture, or composition of matter, or any *new* and *useful* improvement thereof. Over the years, interpretations by the courts have developed the criterion that an invention, to be patentable, must have required ingenuity or skill or imagination beyond that normally expected from a person who is reasonably skillful in that particular line of endeavor.

Patents are sometimes criticized because they are "monopolies." To describe a patent as a monopoly is as wrong as to describe one's ownership of a house as a monopoly. A patent is a governmental recognition of an inventor's ownership of an invention that the inventor has proved to be new and useful, in return for the inventor's agreement that the invention will be published in the form of a patent and that his or her ownership of the invention will be relinquished to the public after a limited period (now 17 years). In the United States the life of a patent *cannot be extended*. A patent is not a monopoly, but it can be used to create a monopoly. So can money, or anything else of value.

Copyrights

A copyright is a grant to an author of the exclusive right, subject to certain limitations, to reproduce copies of a copyrighted work, to prepare derivative works, to distribute copies, and to perform or display audio-visual works publicly.

Copyrights are not so often criticized as being monopolies, although they also constitute intellectual property. There is a dichotomy in academia with regard to copyrighted material. Authors who prepare such material clearly want it to be published or produced. Whether they realize it or not, this means that publishers or producers must recoup their expenses (plus earn a profit unless they operate in the nonprofit sector). Unauthorized copying, which reduces the income of publishers and producers, thus becomes a serious threat. However, teachers and librarians in universities want the widest possible dissemination at the lowest possible cost, so copying without restriction becomes most desirable. But if nothing is published or produced because income is insufficient, there will be nothing to copy. The new copyright law (Public Law 94-553), the first in many years, may adequately balance these interests.

Relations with Faculty and Staff

Industrial and commercial organizations, as part of their conditions of employment, normally take title to intellectual property produced by their employees, either without additional compensation or for a nominal payment. The basic reason for such a practice is in part, sometimes in large part, that a person is employed to create intellectual property and that his or her salary and promotions depend on the amount and/or quality produced. In many companies inventions are the lifeblood of their existence; the same is true for copyrightable material, but generally in different kinds of commercial organizations.

Universities are in a different situation. Their faculties and other personnel are not employed, promoted, or advanced based on the expected or realized monetary value of patented inventions. While they are certainly expected to write, and their writings may be copyrighted, their employment, promotion, or advancement, as mentioned above, is not often based on the monetary value of copyrighted works. Generally, therefore, patentable inventions and copyrightable material cannot in equity be said to belong to a university because of the payment of the salaries of personnel, so other considerations become necessary.

Patent Policy

A patent policy is essential for any university having a significant volume of research activity; many such universities do have patent policies. The reasons for and scope of such policies can be stated as follows:

"Universities by their very nature and by their charters have an obligation to serve the public interest. They do this in a variety of ways in a variety of endeavors. In order to do it effectively in the patent area, universities need to have a patent program which will make patentable inventions available in the public interest under conditions that will promote effective development and utilization." *

In order to fulfill the role described above, a statement of patent policy should set forth the objectives to be achieved and, either as part of the policy itself or as a separate statement, the program that will be followed in order that the objectives will in fact be accomplished. Following is a discussion of the objectives that a reasonable university patent policy should have.

A first objective is to encourage research into any area of interest and promise without regard to potential gain from patent royalties or other such income. This is not to say, however, that a portion of any royalties received may not be returned, as most institutions do, in part to the inventor and in part to the department or program in which the invention arose that earned the royalties. What it does say is that royalty-sharing to either the inventor or the department should not be in such amounts that it will significantly affect the research performed or act as an incentive to other research.

A second objective is that inventions resulting from university research should be made available in the public interest under conditions that will promote their effective development and utilization. This is now generally known as having a technology transfer capability. Several aspects are involved. Some academicians have maintained that the public interest

---

* Testimony by R. J. Woodrow before Subcommittee on Domestic and International Scientific Planning and Analysis of the House Committee on Science and Technology, September 23, 1976.

obligation of all universities is served by publishing in the open literature the results of their research, whether or not this discloses an invention. However, there is an increasing realization in universities and in some parts of government that publication is often not enough to meet the public interest obligation. Furthermore, if publication is the objective, a patent is a well-recognized form of publication. The framers of the Constitution encouraged publication by granting exclusive rights to an inventor but for only a *limited period,* rather than treating inventions as trade secrets, which may never be published.

Most inventions that originate in a university are not practicable in the sense that they can be made available to the public in the form in which they are conceived or reduced to practice in the university. Universities generally do not have the means to develop an invention to a point where it can be produced and marketed. As a result, most university inventions require investments, sometimes millions of dollars, to develop them to a point of practical use and to make them available to the public. Any organization making such an investment should properly insist on some kind of protection, which a patent gives, so that someone else cannot appropriate and market the perfected product without having incurred the costs of developing it to that point. Thus, universities must license their inventions to organizations that will put them to use, and this requires a technology transfer capability, as discussed later in this chapter.

A third objective is to insure, to the extent practical, that inventions resulting from university research will not be used to the detriment of the public interest by the unnecessary exclusion of any qualified user or by any other means. Universities have an obligation to serve the public interest. In the patent field this means, in part, that a patent should be licensed on a *nonexclusive* basis if an exclusive license is not required to interest a licensee in taking an invention and bringing it to market. When an exclusive license is needed, this objective means that the period of exclusivity should run only long enough for the licensee to bring the patented invention to market and earn a reasonable return on the investment. (In some cases licenses may be limited as to fields of application, so that licensees with expertise in other fields of application can use the invention for another kind of product.) Other sorts of protection of the public interest include requirements for licensees to exercise diligence in development and marketing an invention, and reasonable pricing.

A fourth objective of a patent policy is to establish the respective equities of the university and its personnel with regard to patentable inventions. Sometimes the university's equity is set forth in an agreement signed by faculty and staff at the time of employment or at the time of participation in a project; sometimes it is not set forth at all (see later section in this chapter). If the reasoning stated at the beginning of this chapter is valid, a university's equity in inventions in terms of relations with faculty and staff does not arise because of the payment of salary. It must arise, therefore, if it arises at all, from the provision of funds and facilities for the development or reduction to practice of an invention (to obtain a patent, utility and workability of an invention must be proved, which generally but not always means some development or actual reduction to practice). Carrying this reasoning through to its logical conclusion, a university should have no equity (in terms of relations with faculty and staff) in an invention that is intellectually conceived by a member of the faculty or staff and for which the university provided no funds or facilities for development or reduction to practice. A patent policy ought reasonably to apply to students as well as staff, and here (except for employed students) it can be only the provision of funds and facilities that gives the university an equity.

A fifth objective is to advance and encourage the university's purposes with funds accruing to the institution from its equity in inventions. Funds realized by a university from inventions (other than those funds paid to the inventor) are used in a variety of ways; in most institutions the departments in which an invention arose are guaranteed or given preferential treatment for either all or a substantial portion of net royalties received. As stated with reference to the first objective, a guaranteed portion to a department could have unfortunate consequences if by chance, remote though it may be, a very high-paying invention should be made. Any other income is probably best distributed by a research council or other organization that distributes the university's "free" research funds.

A sixth objective is to provide adequate recognition, equity, and *incentive* to inventors by a share in any royalties earned on their inventions since, as stated earlier, university salary scales are rarely based on the expectation of income from inventions. The incentive is necessary so that inventors will disclose inventions, work with patent attorneys, and assist licensees. Shares to inventors usually range from 15% to 50% of net income earned for those inventions in which the university has a normal equity, i.e., where university-provided funds or facilities are used for development or reduction to practice. In recent years there has been a trend toward higher royalties for inventors. At the same time there appears to be some increase in a practice of scaling down from a high initial percentage for inventors (such as 50%) to lower percentages as the total income from an invention increases. There is merit in this practice, since it can avoid an unhealthy bonanza to the inventor, which would inevitably affect his or her colleagues, especially those working together on the project that gave rise to the invention. Inventions that do not use funds or facilities provided by the university for development or reduction to practice, but that are referred to the university for handling, should in terms of equity provide a larger portion of royalties to the inventors.

Patent Relations with Sponsors

All government sponsors, most industrial sponsors, and some other private sponsors, such as voluntary health agencies, have requirements applying to patentable inventions resulting from research that they fund through either grants or contracts. These requirements often do not take into consideration the nature of universities and university research, the objectives a university has in its patent policies, the equities of the university and its personnel in inventions, and the importance of technology transfers if university inventions are to be useful and made available to the public.

Government sponsors' awareness of the special position of universities in the patent field is growing. However, that awareness and the action that can result continually need to be stimulated. The argument carrying the greatest weight is that no one will make the private investment needed to translate the professor's brainchild into a marketable product unless patent protection for the investment is available. In addition, the professor is not interested in making an invention disclosure, lengthy discussion with a patent attorney, and essential but time-consuming advice to a developer unless there is the potential of a royalty or other compensation. The university's equity is not recognized, either, should the government take title to the invention, as it often does. The university's equity is represented by its provision of facilities, almost always some share of the costs, and a large investment in highly competent persons without which no government grant or contract would have been issued. The government's equity as a result of its financing the research should generally be satisfied with a nonexclusive, royalty-free license to practice (or to have practiced) the invention for federal government purposes.

Evidence of the growing concern of government for patentable inventions resulting from grants and contracts to universities is demonstrated by institutional patent agreements that are increasingly provided by federal agencies. These agreements normally cover *all* inventions made under *all* research projects sponsored by the agency involved. To obtain such institutional patent agreements, it is essential that a university have a patent policy approved by the sponsoring agency, together with a capability for identification of inventions, patent application, licensing and monitoring, or in other words, a technology transfer capability. These agreements typically have many requirements that apply to the university in its internal operations and also many requirements that must be accepted by an organization that accepts a license covering an invention resulting from research sponsored by the agency. Under the agreement the government receives among other things a royalty-free, nonexclusive license to inventions plus "march-in" rights, which are the rights for the government to require additional licensees if necessary in the public interest. For agencies not using an institutional patent agreement, a variety of arrangements are possible, based on regulations and negotiations, but they are generally less favorable to the institution.

Industrial sponsors of research, because there are so many more of them and each one has so relatively few relationships with universities, are much less apt to be familiar with or understand university research policies and procedures. Considerable care and effort are therefore necessary in negotiating the terms of research grants and contracts if a university is to attain the objectives recited above insofar as patents and inventions are concerned. The best starting point is a carefully written university statement of terms and conditions that fulfill these objectives, with the understanding that negotiation may lead to some alterations, as mutually agreed upon. (The same written statement can also include acceptable terms as to publication along the lines discussed in chapter 2, since patents and publication are probably the two most difficult points for negotiation in industry grants and contracts.)

As in the case of government grants and contracts, the advancement and protection of the public interest, inventor equities, and university equities should be of primary concern in the negotiation of terms and conditions for patentable inventions in industry grants and contracts. One of the major tasks of technology transfers, namely, selection of a licensee, is generally made unnecessary, since the industrial sponsor takes this role. The precepts stated under the third objective should, if followed, protect the public interest. The university's equity may be waived, but then some other form of compensation could reasonably be requested, such as a payment in excess of costs (some institutions accomplish this by charging a higher indirect cost rate). University negotiators should take care that they do not negotiate away inventors' equities without substantive compensation.

Other sponsors include state and local governments, private foundations, voluntary health agencies, etc. There is such a variety of postures adopted by these sponsors with regard to patentable inventions that it is impossible to generalize, other than to state that the objectives of a university patent policy should prevail to the extent possible.

Patents—Technology Transfer

The term "technology transfer" as used in this chapter refers solely to the process of disclosing, patenting, and licensing of an invention and does not include, as is sometimes the case elsewhere, the transfer (except as it involves an invention) of know-how, processes, ideas, scientific principles, etc. Five basic steps are involved in the process of technology transfer.

1. An invention should be properly and promptly disclosed by the inventor. Obtaining disclosure is probably one of the most difficult tasks university management faces in the patent area. Some other organizations employ patent attorneys or persons of comparable skills to search the notebooks of scientists and engineers to insure that all inventions are disclosed. In most universities the principle of academic freedom would inhibit such a practice. One solution is an adequate royalty percentage for the inventor, as discussed earlier. Another that has worked well is a series of seminars, repeated periodically, to explain what patentable inventions are, how they should be handled, and so forth.

2. After disclosure, there must be an invention evaluation to determine whether there is indeed a patentable invention or merely an improvement that one might expect from somebody reasonably skilled in the particular art, in which case it is rarely patentable. An invention evaluation also involves a forecast of the extent to which patent protection can be obtained, since very narrow patent protection usually means that a patent can be circumvented without too much trouble. In addition, the utility and probable market should be estimated. A patent search may be necessary in order to determine the novelty of the invention as compared with other inventions already patented.

3. The next step is filing a patent application. This is a costly process, since a patent attorney is always required. The broader the claims, the more valuable the patent generally is. In many cases, the U.S. Patent Office rejects the first application, necessitating a second and perhaps even a third or more. The question of foreign patent applications should be considered, and such applications generally must be filed within one year from the date of U.S. application. As pointed out in the section "Publication and Dissemination of Results" in chapter 2, many foreign patent applications

are barred entirely unless the U.S. application has been filed before *any* publication has taken place. Government sponsors must normally be notified when patents are applied for.

4. A licensee or licensees must be located and licenses negotiated. This requires specialized knowledge and expertise to match an invention with the potential interests of an industrial or commercial organization and to be at least somewhat familiar with the licensing practices, including royalties, in that segment of the industrial and commercial economy. The patent policy objectives discussed earlier in this chapter apply particularly at this stage.

5. Finally, a licensee for a patented invention should be monitored, at least to some extent, to ascertain if there is sufficient diligence in development and marketing and also to insure that there is no infringement on the patent by those who are not licensed. The preferred approach when universities hold title to a patent is to place the responsibility for monitoring patent infringement on licensees in a license agreement, since they are strongly motivated against infringement.

Three basic routes, each with possible variations, can be followed in taking the above steps:

The *inventor route* involves the inventor's taking all five steps, although generally in accordance with the approval or direction of the university, depending on provisions of the patent policy.

The *university route* requires that the invention be assigned to the university or to an affiliated research foundation (which for purposes of this chapter is considered a part of the university). The inventor must obviously take step one to disclose the invention, but the university takes the rest, although inventor cooperation is essential in all but step five.

The *patent management organization route* involves assignment of the invention, after inventor disclosure, to an organization such as Research Corporation, University Patents Inc., or Battelle Development Corporation. These organizations operate under an agreement with the institution and handle all necessary measures to accomplish steps two through five, as well as sharing royalties with the institution. Universities having only a few inventions find this to be a preferred route, because of the cost involved in maintaining a competent in-house operation.

Some universities make a practice of uniformly following only one of the routes described above. Some desire more flexibility, and many have a preference for one or another, but do not make an ironclad rule. The more flexible procedure has advantages.

Copyright Policy

Behind any patented invention there is an idea, and the patent covers the idea, no matter what form it takes. A copyright, on the other hand, covers the form or manner in which an idea is expressed, and the same idea can be expressed in a different form or manner, against which a copyright provides no protection. The differences between patents and copyrights in these respects account largely for the differences in policies and practices.

Many more universities have adopted patent policies than have adopted copyright policies. This seems strange when one considers the fact that so many more copyrightable materials, compared with patentable inventions, have been and are being produced in universities. Some of the strangeness disappears when one realizes that the much larger amount of copyrightable material, and the greater number of individuals and disciplines involved, may make the subject of a copyright policy more sensitive and harder to generalize than a patent policy. Traditional practices, including the cry for academic freedom, also militate against a formal policy. What has probably been the impetus in recent years for copyright policies is the increasing variety of material subject to copyright. These include:

"1. Books, journal articles, texts, glossaries, bibliographies, study guides, laboratory manuals, syllabi, tests, and proposals.
   2. Lectures, musical or dramatic compositions, and unpublished scripts.
   3. Films, film strips, charts, transparencies, and other visual aids.
   4. Video and audio tapes and cassettes.
   5. Live video or audio broadcasts.
   6. Programmed instruction materials.
   7. Computer programs.
   8. Other materials." *

The objectives considered desirable in terms of a university copyright policy are discussed below in much the same way that the objectives of a patent policy were discussed.

A first objective is to encourage the preparation of copyrightable material, without emphasis on potential gain from royalties or other income. Members of the faculty and staff have the right to write and should be encouraged to do so. Far from earning royalties, some types of publication, such as page charges for scientific journals, require a subsidy. Universities should be prepared to provide the necessary subsidies and to grant them

---

* "Copyrights at Colleges and Universities: Guidelines for the Development of Policies and Procedures" (Washington, D.C.: Committee on Governmental Relations, National Association of College and University Business Officers, 1972).

reasonably freely. Journals review articles submitted and accept only those worthy of publication, which does provide a certain amount of screening to justify a subsidy. Other types of publication may require more careful review before a subsidy is paid. Page charges for journal articles are generally accepted as a direct cost in government projects.

A second objective is to establish the respective equities of the university and its personnel with regard to copyrightable material; these generally fall into three categories. First, there is material produced with only incidental use of university funds (salary excepted) and the support normally available because of an individual's position in the university (such as office and library), in which case few universities claim any equity. Second, there is the situation in which significant costs to the university are involved in developing copyrightable material, and in this case it is often but not always recognized that the university has an equity, and this equity is realized either by a royalty-sharing arrangement or by reimbursement to the university, out of any royalties received, for the costs involved. The third situation, which does not arise often, is that of a person who may be assigned or may be specifically employed to develop and prepare certain copyrightable material; in this case, royalty sharing is sometimes used, but more often the university claims all the royalties.

A third objective is to advance and encourage research and scholarly endeavor in the university with any funds accruing to the university from copyrights. This is similar to the fifth objective for patents, and its fulfillment should probably be similar.

Copyright Relations with Sponsors

Copyright relations with sponsors are generally not as much of a problem in research grants and contracts as they are in areas like educational services and curriculum development. The government may ask for a royalty-free license to publish, translate, reproduce, deliver, perform, and dispose of (and to authorize others to do so) all copyrighted material resulting from the research. Some sponsors, both government and private, have been known to refuse the right to copyright, either statutory or at common law, which can mean that publication is difficult or impossible, and that parts of what has been written can be taken out of context for unauthorized purposes. Government agencies at times claim ownership to all technical data, including reports, memoranda, notebooks, and even graduate student theses; faculty notebooks and student theses are particularly sensitive areas.

Organizations that represent a number of universities can and do negotiate for the improvement of these conditions. Individual institutions can often do more than they have by appealing at a higher level than the opposite side's negotiators.

Copyrights—Transfer to the Public

Copyrightable materials consisting of manuscripts or other written items are so familiar to universities and their staffs that they need little discussion. Compared with inventions, where only the inventor can apply for a patent (even though it may then be assigned), copyrights are issued to the author or to his or her assignee by payment of a nominal sum and registering the copyright with the U.S. Copyright Office. Most often the copyright or right to copyright is assigned to the publisher.

Other types of copyrightable materials, such as audiovisual material and computer programs, are less familiar and may be more complicated to handle. Different registration forms may be required by the U.S. Copyright Office. There is no publisher and often no party to take a publisher's place. In fact, the institution (sometimes even the author, with the university's consent) may find itself ending up willy-nilly as the organization marketing the material. Sometimes a licensing procedure, as for patents, proves useful. In this area, there are few specifics that apply generally.

Patent and Copyright Agreements

Patent and copyright agreements, as the terms are used here, mean agreements to do all things necessary to comply with the patent and copyright policies of the university and to comply with all patent and copyright requirements of any grant or contract in which the signer participates. It needs to be noted that sponsor requirements as to patents and copyrights generally extend to every person who participates in a project, not only to persons whose compensation is paid by the project. Thus, these requirements apply to those whose salary represents mandatory or voluntary cost sharing and to graduate students who participate while holding a fellowship.

There are wide variations in the practices followed by universities with regard to patent and copyright agreements. Some institutions obtain no such agreements from personnel and rely on the existence of patent and copyright policies (to the extent they do exist), in which case the obligations to the university or to a sponsor may be difficult to enforce. Some institutions obtain only patent agreements. Others may obtain patent and copyright agreements only from those who are paid from sponsored research grants and contracts without covering persons (such as faculty and students) who participate without pay. Then there are some that, to cover all possibilities, obtain agreements from everybody, including students. Further variations also occur.

Some universities, possibly many, might have difficulty in complying with requirements of sponsored grants and contracts. The effective implementation of their own patent and copyright policies, if they have them, could be jeopardized. Each institution in this situation should review its practices.

An important matter that must be decided in preparing patent and copyright agreements (and the same subject is generally covered in patent and copyright policies themselves) is whether the university is always to take title to patentable inventions and copyrightable material or is to take an alternative course of controlling or approving the assignment or licensing of such intellectual property. There is something to be said for the second course, even where it is the normal practice of the institution to take title to patents and copyrights, since other situations can arise (such as when the government takes title to an invention) when the extra red tape of institutional involvement in the assignment chain is not warranted. When the university uses another organization for patent management, direct assignment from the inventor to that organization is obviously simpler. Some universities have a policy of not taking title to patents because, among other things, they do not want to become involved in patent litigation. As far as copyrights are concerned, licenses are less frequent than for patents and the copyright is most often assigned to a publisher, or the publisher itself may take out the copyright.

Finally, the question arises as to whether there should be separate personnel agreements for patents and for copyrights, or a single agreement for both. This is an administrative decision that depends largely on the spectrum of individuals who are required to sign. Patent agreements, which can generally be confined to persons who might reasonably be expected to make an invention, would not normally be needed for the humanities and social sciences, for which copyright agreements may be particularly important. The reverse, however, is not true, since scientists and engineers also generate copyrightable material.

On balance, a single agreement for both patents and copyrights seems preferable, with all faculty, professional personnel, and graduate students asked to sign. An attorney should prepare the agreement, whose elements might include recitation to the effect that the signer, in consideration of funds and facilities provided by the university for the conduct of research and other scholarly activities, agrees to:

1. Compliance with the patent policy and copyright policy of the

university, whose provisions have been brought to the attention of the signer (this assumes that the policies state whether or not the university is assigned title or has other types of control).

2. Prompt disclosure of any inventions conceived or first reduced to practice in the course of university research.

3. Disclosure of income realized from copyrighted materials whose preparation required significant university costs other than the payment of salary or stipends or normally provided facilities such as office space and library.

4. Compliance with requirements of any sponsored grant or contract in which the signer participates to the extent that those requirements pertain to inventions, copyrightable material, or technical data.

7

Indirect Costs

INDIRECT COSTS BECAME A BONE OF CONTENTION ALMOST AS SOON AS THE words were introduced into the vocabulary of university research. This occurred during and after World War II, when the government first became active in sponsoring such research. Misunderstandings on the subject are common among faculty members, department chairmen, deans, presidents, and sometimes even business officers. The "distribution" of indirect cost reimbursements is debated. Program officers in government agencies and in private sponsoring organizations frequently do not understand the subject. Congressional committees are often confused.

At the heart of many misunderstandings is the failure to realize that indirect costs are *real costs* of a project to which they are assigned, just as real as the direct costs of the salaries of persons employed on the project or the supplies bought for the project. Indirect costs are computed in accordance with government cost principles, as stated in Office of Management and Budget (OMB) Circular A-21, also known as Federal Management Circular FMC 73-8; indirect costs are *audited* and *approved* by the government for allocation to government projects. As stated in a monograph "Indirect Costs in Universities," "Without [adequate] indirect costs, research in universities would as surely fail as if there were no direct cost support." *

Concepts and Principles

It has been said that indirect costs are a group of approximations based on a reasoned assumption. This is largely true, and the assumption applies also to organizations other than universities, including industry and not-for-profits. To quote further from the monograph mentioned above, the assumption requires the definition of two kinds of costs:

"1. *Direct costs* are those which can be identified and charged to a specific project relatively easily with a reasonable degree of accuracy and

---

* R. J. Woodrow, "Indirect Costs in Universities," Administrative Service Supplement 4:5:1 (Washington, D.C.: National Association of College and University Business Officers, 1976), pp. 1-2.

65

without an inordinate amount of accounting. Examples include such items as the salary of a technician working full-time on a project, or the purchase of chemicals for the project, or travel costs for the purpose of the project, or computer time billed to the project.

"2. *Indirect costs,* in contrast with direct costs, are those that have been incurred for purposes common to a number or all of the specific projects, programs, or activities of an institution but which cannot be identified and charged directly to such projects, programs, or activities relatively easily with a reasonable degree of accuracy and without an inordinate amount of accounting. Examples include such items as heating, lighting, air conditioning, and janitorial services of buildings, and administrative services such as accounting, purchasing, personnel, and library services.

"The assumption is that the indirect costs associated with or benefiting in some way a group of projects, programs, or activities (hereafter referred to as projects) can equitably be prorated to a specific project in proportion to its size in relation to the size of all affected projects.
Thus,

(a) indirect costs for project = $\dfrac{\text{(indirect costs of all projects)} \times \text{(size of project)}}{\text{size of all projects}}$

If we define

(b) indirect cost rate = $\dfrac{\text{indirect costs for all projects}}{\text{size of all projects}}$

then

(c) total cost of project = direct costs of project + indirect cost rate × size of project.

"The relative size of projects, both for the the determination of an indirect cost rate in (b) above and for the application of the rate in (c), is almost always measured in terms of some part or all of the direct costs of the projects, although other forms of measurement are possible. Such other forms of measurement could be population, full-time equivalents, square feet of space used, or number of purchase orders issued. In fact, some of these measures are used not for the measurement of project size, but for the allocation of overall activity costs such as libraries and operation and maintenance of physical plant.

"The three most commonly used measures of size of projects, generally called the base or bases, are:

1. Total direct salaries.
2. Total direct salaries plus personnel benefits.
3. Total direct costs (generally excluding capital costs and major subcontracts). . . . .

"It seems obvious that the indirect cost rate in (b) will be significantly lower if total direct costs are used as the base or measure of size than if total direct salaries (only a component of total direct costs) are used, *even though the dollar amount of total indirect costs remains the same.* The indirect costs assessed to any one project by formula (c) will be the same or somewhat higher or lower (again, the average will be the same), depending on the project mix of salaries and other direct costs compared with the mix for all projects."

Computation of Indirect Costs

The computation and determination of indirect costs for all projects sponsored by the federal government at universities, not only research projects, are governed by federal government cost principles that are periodically refined and revised. These cost principles are different from those that apply to industry, not-for-profits, and state and local governments. One can say almost with certainty that the cost principles for universities are not as favorable as those for the other kinds of organizations because more costs are disallowed and more methodology is imposed.

Under government cost principles, universities having a limited amount of government-sponsored projects of any kind, such as research or instruction, are permitted to compute indirect costs using an abbreviated method (the "short form"), which is mainly based on their published financial reports. The result is a single averaging rate that applies to all government-sponsored projects including research, instruction, and public service.

However, this sort of averaging is not accepted for institutions having a larger volume of government-sponsored work. For these universities, several categories of direct cost activities must be established (as for instruction, research, auxiliary enterprises, etc.) and a separate indirect cost rate must be computed for each one that contains government-sponsored projects. These separate categories are required because the various elements of indirect costs do not equitably pertain, or may not pertain at all, to each category of direct costs to the same degree.

For the "long form" computation the elements of indirect costs allocated to the several categories of direct costs are listed below. The basis of allocation (direct salaries, total direct costs, or square feet occupied, etc.) for one element may be different from that of another element, and the categories to which the elements are allocated may be different.

1. *Depreciation or use allowances for buildings* are allowable costs so that original investments may be recovered over useful lives and funds may be accumulated to pay for replacement or renovation. A use allowance is a rather special term often employed for universities in lieu of depreciation.

2. *Depreciation or use allowances for equipment* are allowable costs so that original investments may be recovered over useful lives and funds may be accumulated to pay for replacement. No depreciation or use allowance can be claimed for equipment (or buildings) paid for by the government.

3. *Operation and maintenance costs* for buildings and grounds include utilities, janitorial services, routine maintenance and repairs, etc.

4. *Departmental administration costs* include salaries and expenses for deans, department heads, other administrative personnel, secretarial services consistently charged, office expenses, and other costs involved at a school or departmental level that are administrative.

5. *Student administration and student services* include deans of students, registrars, student health services, etc.

6. *Library costs* include the cost of books and other library materials together with library operating costs.

7. *Research administration costs* cover costs for functions such as those listed in chapter 3, together with similar costs for nonresearch projects, depending on the administrative structure.

8. *General administration and general expenses* include all offices and costs so identified for a president on down. Government cost principles make some of these costs, such as fund raising, unallowable as indirect costs for government projects.

Indirect costs are derived by determining the total indirect costs allocated from elements 1 through 8 above to each of the direct cost categories of instruction, research, etc. and then dividing the total allocated from those elements by the direct cost base, i.e., direct salaries, direct salaries plus benefits, or modified total direct costs included in each category. As may be inferred from what was said earlier, some of the thorniest problems arise during the allocation process, where each indirect cost element must be properly distributed to each affected direct cost category in such a way that benefits and costs are in similar proportions.

In addition to the basic direct cost categories for functions like instruction, research, and auxiliary enterprises, separate indirect cost rates are frequently required for what can be called subcategories of the main categories and which do not use, or are not equitably allocated, indirect costs in the same proportions. Examples of some of the kinds of situations in which other indirect cost rates *may* be required are:

1. Off-campus projects.
2. Separate campuses.
3. Medical or agricultural centers.
4. Projects using government buildings.
5. Projects in which significant types of normally indirect costs (like operation and maintenance or purchasing) are charged as direct.
6. Large, self-contained laboratories.

Audit, Negotiation, and Application

Indirect cost computation, once completed, must be submitted to a "cognizant" government agency for audit and negotiation. The Department of Health, Education, and Welfare has cognizance over most universities, but other agencies are involved for other universities. For major institutions the audit is generally conducted on site, but for institutions not so large the audit representatives may only review the computation submitted at their home office. An audit is neither a negotiation (although some negotiation may be involved) nor a determination of the rates that will necessarily be accepted. If an institution believes it is being unfairly handled, it has the right and should invoke that right to appeal any decision made, in accordance with an accepted appeals procedure.

Once indirect cost rates have been negotiated, based on costs for a particular year, they are usually applied as fixed rates to a subsequent year or years, often with a roll-forward provision so that any over- or under-recovery from a previous year will be added to or subtracted from indirect costs incurred for a subsequent year. Sometimes used instead of fixed rates, provisional rates with retroactive adjustments to actual costs incurred create problems, either because there must be retroactive credits to the government if actual rates are lower than provisional rates or because of generally unsuccessful attempts to collect additional payments should the actual computed rates exceed the provisional rates billed.

Incremental Indirect Cost Rates

From the inception, after World War II, of the practice of charging some costs for research as direct costs and others as indirect costs, there have been proponents both inside and outside of universities for the concept of "incremental" costs, which economists often refer to as "marginal" costs. The argument is that a research project of small or moderate size, when added to a university research program totaling millions of dollars, should have an indirect cost rate lower than the average, because the incremental or marginal indirect costs are proportionately lower than average. However, there are several problems with this argument:

1. The economists' marginal costs generally apply in the case of capital-intensive industries, where capital costs for facilities and equipment are a major factor in total costs. In these cases, volume can increase appreciably without a corresponding increase in costs, since capital costs do not have to be increased. However, universities are generally accepted as a very labor-intensive industry, since capital costs are only a small fraction of total costs. The marginal cost theory thus has little application.

2. Admittedly, there are step functions in indirect costs as total research volume increases; these may be in small steps like the addition of an item of equipment or in larger steps like a new building. But the problems of using these steps in the determination of incremental indirect cost rates can be illustrated by the example of a university's having a telephone switchboard containing only one open connection remaining. A new research project uses that last connection. The next project necessitates installation of a new switchboard, telephone operator, and possibly a building addition. It would be unfair and unreasonable to charge the first project nothing for switchboard costs and charge the second project for the entire new switchboard and associated costs. Averaging is the only answer.

3. Indirect costs are sometimes denied because they are so difficult to identify with individual projects; sometimes, in fact, they are only second-order effects. A sponsor such as a private foundation may say that a president's office is going to be there anyway, so why should part of it be paid for by the sponsored project? In the first place, such a tiny part of the president's office is assigned to the project that it may seem meaningless, until one realizes that the indirect costs allocated to any one project are made up of many, mostly tiny pieces. Second, the president may never be involved with that project at all, but is deeply concerned with the development and implementation of policies, procedures, and organization that affect the project. Thus, the total of all projects, each with a tiny effect of its own, when added together, has clearly placed an added burden on the president's office to the extent that it has diminished the effort devoted to other undertakings. Such undertakings should then not continue to be assessed the same costs as before, or otherwise staff and costs will have expanded by the addition of new positions or in other ways. Thus, each project ought to pay its properly allocated share.

4. Finally, the federal government does not accept (at least officially) the incremental or marginal indirect cost philosophy. Indirect costs must be assessed to *all* research projects on the same basis unless, as discussed earlier in this chapter, there are major differences in the type or amount of indirect cost services provided, as for off-campus projects or large research centers. As a result, a research project financed by a private foundation, for example, which does not properly reimburse full indirect costs, will be assessed those costs anyway, which means that those costs cannot be reassessed and recovered from other projects. The university must absorb the indirect costs, which would be largely paid for by other projects were the foundation project not present.

Direct versus Indirect Costs

One of the most important factors determining the indirect cost rate or rates at a university is the extent to which certain types of costs are treated as direct costs or as indirect costs. Government cost principles allow considerable flexibility in this regard. There can be said to be two opposing philosophies.

One philosophy claims that the more that costs are charged directly to sponsored research, the greater will be the percentage of total costs recovered. This will certainly be true if there are low sponsor *limits* on indirect cost rates reimbursed, such as used to be the case but is no longer for government-sponsored research, although the limitation still exists for government-sponsored instruction, as well as for projects sponsored by many private organizations like foundations. This philosophy may also be applicable in the sense of who gets the money, as for state institutions in which reimbursements for indirect costs may follow a different channel and be subject to different controls than reimbursements for direct costs incurred. The manager or entrepreneur position that principal investigators enjoy in university research inclines them towards wanting control over as many costs as possible; this objective can be best achieved by as much direct costing as possible, since a principal investigator's control over indirect costs is only marginal or nonexistent. For example, if secretarial support is a direct charge, then principal investigators can decide how much project money to spend on this function; if secretarial support is an indirect charge, then someone else generally has the final say.

However, there is another philosophy stating that work is more efficiently performed and *total* costs are less if similar services are not segmented into bits and pieces, each to be charged individually and as direct costs. There are some obvious examples, such as buildings with central heating, utilities, and air conditioning. Central research administration, purchasing, and personnel, *if these provide effective and efficient service to research* (see chapter 8), are other examples. The same is true, at least to some extent, for libraries and other elements of indirect costs.

With respect to these two philosophies, which have an important impact on how a university is organized for research, one word is becoming increasingly important in government principles and regulations with regard to accounting for costs in government-sponsored projects; that word is *consistency*. Emerson said, "Foolish consistency is the hobgoblin of little minds." But *reasonable* consistency is essential in the matter of direct versus indirect costing. The government's Cost Accounting Standards Board has stated that "all costs incurred for the same purpose, in like circumstances, are either direct costs *only* or indirect costs *only* with respect to final cost objectives" (emphasis added).* To illustrate:

1. If secretarial or administrative personnel are made a direct charge to sponsored research, no secretaries or administrators can be charged to the departmental administration element of indirect costs, except to the extent that they serve the *overall* administrative function of the department. In other words, secretaries cannot be made a direct charge to research projects while other secretaries employed for instructional purposes are treated as part of the departmental administration element of indirect costs. The same applies to office supplies, telephones, etc.

2. If a research administration office (or an affiliated foundation) provides services such as accounting, purchasing, and personnel, and the cost of those services is allocated to research projects, then the cost of that type of service cannot be allocated to those research projects as part of the general administration and general expense element of indirect costs.

3. If a part of normal operation and maintenance expenses, or a building paid for by the government, or a significant number of library-type books are made a direct charge to the project or projects, then there must be an appropriate adjustment in the indirect cost rate.

The adjustments listed as examples, as well as others that may be required, can become complicated. It is almost an axiom that the amount of accounting needed increases as the amount of direct costing increases, at least up to a point. This is part of the reason for the increased efficiency of treating more costs as indirect, if the second philosophy is to be believed. Another factor contributing to the problem is in the character of people;

---

* Part 402—Cost Accounting Standard—"Consistency in Allocating Costs Incurred for the Same Purpose," Cost Accounting Standards Board, Washington, D.C. See *Federal Register,* vol. 41, no. 119 (June 18, 1977).

principal investigators are less apt to share staff, services, or equipment if these are a direct charge to their projects. Such sharing also complicates the problem of accounting at the investigator's level. This type of accounting problem may enter in even more heavily when a departmental administrator has the thankless task of accounting for his or her time split among ten projects and other departmental functions as well.

There may be too much emphasis on direct costing in some universities. It results in there being much less of a cohesive bond as far as the university is concerned. Basically, it is less efficient, and the many little islands of direct cost enterprises encourage divisiveness.

Precision

Precision is the sine qua non of accountants. It is important in assigning direct costs to research projects, but precision is not consistency. And precision is, by definition, not achievable in indirect costs. As should be evident from the formulas set out earlier in this chapter, indirect cost rates *average* the indirect costs over many projects in a way that is expected to give reasonably equitable treatment to each, but that cannot be proved exactly for any one.

Government agencies have been known to emphasize precision to the extent that one whole segment of costs is disregarded because its cost-benefit relationship with government-sponsored research cannot be precisely measured. Universities have also been at fault in maintaining laboriously measured numbers for some kinds of indirect cost allocations, such as square feet for allocating certain types of operation and maintenance costs of physical plant, when those numbers are no more meaningful than simpler approximations.

Equity

Indirect costs may be separated from direct costs in a consistent fashion, and the allowability of costs may be carefully determined, yet the resulting indirect cost rates may provide inequitable reimbursement. It has been argued that equity is served if the total indirect costs for all government projects represent equitable reimbursement to a university. Clearly, this would not be true for the type of situations discussed earlier, such as off-campus projects and large, self-contained laboratories. It is also not true if there are *significant* differences from equitable treatment among projects on the same campus. Even if the total government payment to a university is equitable, individual agencies and parts of those agencies will take a dim view of paying more than their fair share for projects they sponsor, because the projects of other agencies are paying less. More important internally, individual principal investigators at the university may cry that they are being treated unfairly if their projects are getting far less than a fair share of the indirect cost services those projects are paying for. The cries can be heard not only internally but externally as well, in sponsor offices and in the halls of Congress.

The budgetary and resource allocation process in a university has been faulted where the types of inequity described above occur. Long lead times and unchangeable budgets often do not provide the flexibility so important to research endeavors. And principal investigators, without the sort of education discussed later in this chapter, often expect much greater services from the indirect cost elements nearest to them, such as departmental administration or maintenance of their laboratory, than the reimbursement actually covers. Furthermore, each element of indirect costs does not need to be allocated in exactly the same proportion to each project, since some may use proportionately more space or equipment, while others may have greater demands on the library, and so forth.

Notwithstanding these justifications, it is important that all research projects receive reasonably equitable treatment in the allocation of indirect cost services and benefits.

Students

Universities have students, and the fact that they do substantially complicates the computation of indirect cost rates compared with industry or other types of organizations. Students, other than those employed by the institution, do not receive a salary that can serve as part of a base for allocating elements of indirect costs. For example, if all persons occupying a building or buildings are paid a salary, then those salaries can be used as a base for allocating the building depreciation and operation and maintenance costs among those salaries. However, if some of those persons occupying the building are unsalaried students, then the use of salaries as an allocation base does not allocate any building depreciation or operation and maintenance costs to that part of the instruction function represented by the students. As a result, measurements of square feet, or weighting factors, or other types of special analyses, all of which are more complicated, must be used. It should be said, however, that it *is* possible to justify salaries as an allocation base by special studies; the reason that these studies show that salaries are an equitable base is that there is a much higher cost per square foot for research space versus instructional space.

The allocation of library costs to determine a library factor in the indirect cost rate is also complicated by the presence of students. Circulation data on the use of library materials are *not* a good measure of how costs should be allocated. Most librarians maintain that the only reasonable method of allocating library costs is primarily on the basis of the extent of a library collection and its *potential* use, no matter how infrequent that use may be, with circulation a significantly smaller factor in the equation. Students and faculty are not a homogeneous population as far as library needs are concerned.

In addition, there are large elements of what are regularly treated as general administration and general expenses, which require special treatment because they are concerned with students. These include student services and student administration of various kinds. The allocation of a proper share of these costs to government-sponsored research, because students are employed in such research, is a perpetual bone of contention.

Competence and Diligence

Use of the "long form" procedure for computing indirect costs is complicated, so a lack of competence or diligence can lead to inadequate cost recovery; some examples follow. Historical costs and property records to compute depreciation and/or use allowances for buildings and equipment may not be available, or may not be available in proper form. Adequate consideration may not have been given, including consideration of the long-term economic value of money, to the employment of depreciation instead of use allowances for buildings and equipment. No thought may have been given to the use of weighting factors for the much higher costs of building, operating, and maintaining research space. Inadequate surveys may have been made, if any have been made at all, to arrive at the time and the cost of faculty members, in addition to the chairmen, for administrative duties they perform or committees on which they serve. Other departmental costs and expenses may be overlooked. The costs of research administration may be understated by the amount incurred for this purpose in the offices of deans and others. The costs of a library system for research may be measured inadequately, since adequate measurement requires rather sophisticated analyses not based on use alone. These are only some of the examples that can be cited.

Diligence and competence are essential if these problems are to be solved. A system of accounts that parallels the chart of organization, while probably impossible to achieve in all respects, can contribute significantly to the prompt and proper accumulation of costs for an indirect cost rate computation. State-imposed accounting systems, discussed in more detail in chapter 8, can and do create problems. Insofar as the offices gathering information needed for the computation of an indirect cost rate are concerned, a better relationship with faculty and departments needs to be developed in many universities. The assistance of accounting firms or consultants may sometimes be of significantly more value than their cost. Consulting with other universities can help. But a *full knowledge and understanding of the applicable government cost principles are of paramount importance.*

Variations in Indirect Cost Rates

There are wide variations among universities in their indirect cost rates. These variations have been of concern not only within the university community, but also among sponsors, particularly the federal agencies and the Congress. Reasons for the variations, most of which have been discussed earlier in this chapter, include:

1. Differences in the base, with an indirect cost rate based on total direct costs being much lower than one based on salaries, although there is no difference in indirect costs themselves.

2. Differences in function, with indirect cost rates for instruction generally higher than for research because total true costs of instruction are higher.

3. Differences in accounting for costs as direct or indirect, although the total costs of a project will generally be the same.

4. Differences in diligence and competence in determining indirect cost rates.

5. Differences in the amount of indirect cost services provided.

The differences in indirect cost rates cannot be used as a measure of efficiency or inefficiency, or of underpayment or overpayment. There is a strong built-in incentive for efficiency in incurring costs that are treated as indirect, since the university must pay from its own resources that portion of the indirect cost elements that must inevitably be prorated to the portion of the direct cost categories that are the university's financial responsibility. The more that costs are treated as indirect rather than as direct, the greater is the amount that must be prorated between sponsor-financed and university-financed activities. As a result, somewhat similar to what some industries have found, overemphasis on direct costing can lead to less overall efficiency.

Use of Indirect Cost Reimbursements

Indirect costs at universities are costs that have actually been incurred and that have been audited and approved by the federal government in accordance with government-established cost principles. This statement is certainly true for all projects sponsored by the government, and since government-sponsored projects represent a large majority of all sponsored projects at universities, there is a strong presumption that similar accounting practices have been used for all. Since these indirect costs have therefore all been legitimately incurred, the use to which the funds are put once they are reimbursed should be purely academic.

However, there is a story—undoubtedly apocryphal—about a state university president who asked a group of state legislators at a homecoming football game, "How do you like this stadium I built with the indirect costs from government contracts?" One legislator replied, "You didn't build it with government indirect costs; the state paid for it and you didn't get our approval."

The legislator was right. The federal government certainly never audited and approved the costs of the stadium as a part of indirect costs on government projects. What actually happened was that the federal government paid the correct amount for the indirect cost functions that it agreed were properly ascribed to the performance of government projects. However, the state also provided funds for those indirect cost functions. Thus, there were funds left over, which could go to the stadium. The audit trail may have showed that these were funds received from the government. But there are no blue dollars or red dollars; the reason for the excess was the extra state dollars provided.

As stated earlier, the story is undoubtedly apocryphal. However, in state universities there is considerable controversy about the use of indirect cost reimbursements. No state university has been encountered in which there was not *some* distribution of *ostensible* reimbursements for indirect costs for purposes other than which they were generated. The purposes for which such funds are often allocated include fellowships, internal research, equipment, etc. While these allocations can clearly have a salutary effect, they do create problems. Persons outside of the university, including those in the federal agencies and in Congress, who do not fully understand what is happening, can be led to believe that indirect costs are not real costs, but some sort of profit or fee. Persons within the university, faculty members in particular, can come to the same conclusion, but with a different kind of reaction.

For independent institutions, the type of treatment accorded to reimbursement of indirect costs described above has not been encountered. If it does occur somewhere, it is rare, and the amounts involved would undoubtedly be small. In general, the payments for indirect costs received are taken in as general unrestricted income, from which budgetary allocations are made for the indirect cost functions performed.

In chapter 1, under "Institutional Funds for Research," it is indicated that state universities report a substantially greater portion of expenditures for research than do independent institutions from available funds that can be freely used for research purposes. It is more than likely that a significant part of the reason for this greater portion in state universities is the ostensible use of indirect cost reimbursements received from sponsored projects, as described above.

Finally, a few words should be said about the portion of indirect cost reimbursements that are for depreciation or use charges for buildings and equipment; these are not current out-of-pocket expenditures. The concept behind them is, at least in major part, to replenish capital resources that can be used to pay for capital modifications or replacements. The author has inadequate data to prove any particular point, but there is not much evidence to show that all funds received are consistently set aside in reserves. Thus, when capital replacements or modifications are needed, the necessary funds must be either raised or allocated from other resources.

Education

Far too many universities are at fault because they do not communicate to faculty and staff the facts about indirect costs. The misunderstandings that obscure the subject are damaging to both internal and external relations. Damage to external relations occurs in two ways. In the first place, faculty who do not understand indirect costs and think they are unfair communicate their feelings to sponsors, who thus become less than sympathetic to the payment of indirect costs. Second, faculty, either permanently or temporarily, sometimes join the program staffs of sponsors (private agencies in addition to government), where the negative education they were given on indirect costs becomes a detriment to universities seeking project sponsorship. It must be remembered that a faculty member as a principal investigator usually starts out with a predilection against indirect costs, since his or her entrepreneurial instincts run counter to costs over which he or she does not have direct control.

These problems have been alleviated in some universities. The solution is not difficult, but takes time and effort. The process is one of education, which universities—of all organizations—should be able to handle. A basic explanatory memorandum covering indirect costs in general and the application of indirect costs to the particular institution is a good starting point. Seminars with individual departments led by a preceptor who knows the subject are often helpful. An open-door policy can help in answering individual questions. Adequate answers must be available to staff members who state that their project provided so many dollars for a particular indirect cost service, but they never received any of that service.

Education in universities with regard to indirect costs has often been inadequate and needs to be improved.

8

Administrative Offices and Supporting Services and Facilities

ADMINISTRATIVE OFFICES AND SUPPORTING SERVICES AND FACILITIES ARE important constituents for university research. No matter how self-contained a project becomes, administrative functions—such as accounting, purchasing, personnel, and departmental administration—and facilities, such as buildings and equipment, are always necessary. Supporting services in varying degrees of importance, depending on the nature of the research, include libraries, computers, stockrooms, shops, animal centers, and other services. All the above have a significant effect on research performed, whether provided from within the project or from more general university resources.

Almost all the administrative functions and supporting services and facilities mentioned for research are also required for instruction; ostensibly, therefore, universities should be well equipped to provide them. However, the characteristics of the functions, services, and facilities required for much university research are often different from those that may be acceptable for instruction. As a result, modifications may be essential if sufficient flexibility or other features have not been built in. In some state universities where these modifications and adaptations have not been possible for certain functions and services, primarily because of state regulations, separate affiliated but privately incorporated foundations have been established to provide the functions and services (these foundations were mentioned in earlier chapters and are discussed in more detail in chapter 9). That such separate foundations are necessary in some cases is evidence of the need for different ways of handling research requirements.

Earlier chapters mentioned entrepreneurship on the part of principal investigators and that this, along with other factors, can lead to undue emphasis on charging *some* of the functions described above as a direct cost instead of prorating them as an indirect cost. Direct costing is proper and desirable for supporting services such as computers, shops, and stockrooms for which reasonable pricing systems can be devised. Direct costing may also be desirable for certain administrative functions for large, self-contained laboratories or projects, but the principle of consistency and government regulations will then generally require separate indirect cost rates. However, for projects integrated into a departmental or interdisciplinary structure, too much emphasis on direct costing is divisive and inefficient. In other words, university management should be able to provide these functions more effectively than each principal investigator acting on his or her own behalf.

The question of direct versus indirect costing can in some ways be expressed as a question of centralization versus decentralization. Almost every organization of significant size becomes involved sooner or later in deciding to what extent certain administrative and supporting services and functions should be centralized or decentralized; the solution in many cases is a bit of each. Examples will be evident in later parts of this chapter.

Finally, an ingredient of major importance is the concept and attitude of service for administrative offices and supporting functions. One of the most effective business officers visited under the NSF grant referenced in the introduction, and one who is much appreciated by principal investigators at his institution, initiated his interview with words to the effect that he regarded his job as one *primarily* of providing service.

Accounting

A controller's office plays a vital role in the management of a university. The accounts that are established, the ways in which costs and commitments are recorded, the computation of indirect cost rates, and the reporting of costs are far from a complete list of the accounting functions of the typical controller's office, but they are the ones that most directly and intimately affect management for research. Other necessary functions are the payment of research salaries and other costs, and the billing and collection of funds from sponsors.

It is axiomatic that a good accounting structure should be designed to fit an organization, not that the organization must be force-fitted to an accounting configuration. This does not mean that there should not be changes made in organization if accounting can be significantly improved as a result, *and if the performance of work does not suffer.* The close relation between work performed and accounts maintained means that a controller must be knowledgeable in the many things a university does, including at least the general nature of the research performed.

As for specific tasks in the accounting area that heavily affect research, the first is the establishment of accounts *properly coded* for each project that is activated. If accounts are not properly coded—as, for example, for research as compared with other sponsored projects, or for sources of funds such as government, industry, foundations, or internal sources—then the reporting of expenditures in a meaningful manner becomes difficult, if not impossible. It is hard to explain the discrepancies, sometimes large discrepancies, that appear in reports such as the National Science Foundation's "Expenditures for Scientific Activities at Universities and Colleges," mentioned in chapter 1, unless they are due to inaccuracies in coding and accounting for project costs. University management should have numbers of the same kind that are reasonably accurate if management is to do its job. If a single channel through research administration is used for the acceptance and activation of research projects or programs as advocated in chapter 3, and research administration provides the coding, then significant errors should be avoidable.

The second task is adequately accounting for the direct costs of research. Costs must obviously be charged to the proper account, and adequate substantiation of charges must be obtained. This can be particularly burdensome and irritating to faculty and staff if not done with understanding and some consultation, particularly with regard to the time and effort reports required by the federal government for persons whose work is charged to more than one account. Discrepancies must be reconciled between these reports and the somewhat similar personnel reports sometimes required by state agencies, and no avenue should be left unexplored to make the two reports the same. Transfers of costs from one project to another, which are questionable in the eyes of federal auditors, must be justified, although as indicated in chapter 3, it is best for research administration to obtain the justification.

The third task is the computation of indirect cost rates, discussed in detail in chapter 7. It is hard to see how this task can be performed adequately if the coding, accounts, and recording of costs described above are not handled satisfactorily. *Consistency* in accounting for costs as either direct or indirect, as discussed in chapter 7, is particularly important.

The fourth and last task is the provision of accurate and prompt financial reports in the proper format to principal investigators, and also to research administration for the performance of the latter's monitoring function described in chapter 3. The format of a project financial report should correspond with the budget format as approved by the sponsor. Although there are some differences among sponsors, it is not difficult to design a single financial report with an adequate list of categories of costs that accommodates all but a few special cases. A minimum adequate report includes for each category (such as salaries, supplies, travel, indirect costs, etc.) the amount spent during the previous month, the cumulative amount spent since inception, the amount budgeted, and the budgeted funds left unspent. A more complete report also includes *all* the amounts committed but unspent for each category; it is only make-work to include purchase order commitments if the much larger items of salary commitments, together with associated benefits and indirect costs, are omitted. However, subtracting at the outset of a project the *total* amount budgeted for indirect costs, as is sometimes done, can be questioned: it can be taken to mean that management is determined to get *its* share of the money no matter what happens to the project. The best system is to report monthly indirect costs as they are earned.

If principal investigators are to fulfill their responsibilities, which include staying within sponsor-approved budget ceilings and *also* within the amounts allotted to specific categories such as travel and equipment, they need accurate project financial reports promptly. Where their needs have not been adequately met, project bookkeepers or secretaries doubling as bookkeepers have been employed; this is a widespread practice. However, even the best and most timely financial reports may not be sufficient for project-level accounting as, for example, to determine midmonth status. There is promise in a system observed in one university that provides an instantaneous display on the departmental terminal of the financial status of a project when the system is interrogated using the project account number; even here the system will be inadequate if the input information, such as invoices, salaries, etc., is delayed.

Purchasing and Subcontracting

Purchasing and subcontracting mean the same thing for research as they do for other university requirements, but the way in which they need to be performed is often different. Government regulations define subcontracts as including purchase orders. For the purposes of this chapter, and as generally used in many universities, *purchasing* means the acquisition of items on a fixed-price basis; *subcontracting* means the acquisition of goods or services on other than a fixed-price basis, or contractual arrangements for research or development, or other special sorts of arrangements such as the employment of outside consultants.

Why is purchasing different for research than for other university functions? In the first place, quantities are generally small. Second, the item needed is apt to be more highly specialized, often to the extent that there is only one particular article made by one particular manufacturer that will meet the need. And third and most important is the urgency of the need;

since research is an exploration into the *unknown,* its needs cannot be forecast with certainty very far ahead, or perhaps not ahead at all. If an item is needed, then time and money are often wasted until it is available.

University-wide purchasing procedures and purchasing staffs may not provide the services needed for research. Requirements for detailed purchase specifications, written quotations, and competitive bid procedures may need to be altered so that the value of time (and frustration) are taken into consideration. It is for these reasons that a separate purchasing organization for research requirements has been established in some universities. The nearly fifty affiliated foundations that have been established for state universities have often had the problems of state purchasing systems as one major reason for existence.

Every federal government contract requires that certain of the terms and conditions (or boilerplate) of the prime contract be incorporated into all purchase orders and subcontracts. There are a minimum of such requirements for government grants, although these are increasing. A standard purchase order attachment is the easiest way to comply, but a lawyer with knowledge of government contracts should prepare it.

Subcontracts as defined earlier are sometimes handled by the same office that handles purchasing. However, it may be advantageous to have subcontracts prepared and issued by the research administration office responsible for negotiation and administration of the prime contract or grant. Special terms and conditions must generally be inserted similar to those contained in the prime contract or grant, *or in the grant manual.* These vary significantly, depending on the grant or contract, whereas terms and conditions for straight purchase orders rarely do. The types of requirements involved include clauses pertaining to inventions and patents, copyrights and technical data, termination, disputes, litigation, insurance, and more. Also needed for subcontracts on a cost or cost-plus-a-fee basis are the cost principles applicable and, quite important, a provision for final payment by the university only to the extent that the subcontract costs have been audited by a cognizant audit agency. Subcontracts often require administration by the university during the period of performance, and purchasing offices are rarely equipped to provide this service.

Personnel Offices

Personnel offices, as the term is intended here, are concerned with the employment, continuing personnel relations including salary adjustments and promotions, and benefits for what are often called nonacademic personnel. Included in nonacademic personnel are a large group of positions ranging from administrators to groundskeepers. Sometimes this includes nonfaculty professionals, but as indicated in chapter 5, at least the research staff personnel are better handled through the same channels used for the faculty.

In the nonacademic personnel area the types of positions of most immediate concern to research endeavors are secretaries, technicians of all descriptions, and occasionally machinists, glassblowers, draftsmen, and photographers. The services of some of these, such as machinists, are often furnished through central or departmental shops, as discussed later in this chapter. A secretary may be treated as part of departmental administration (and thus as an item of indirect cost). Technicians are right at the core of many projects.

The nature of these jobs and the qualifications required to fill them are often different for research as compared with instruction or any other university function. A personnel office must be attuned to these needs. Furthermore, there is apt to be more turnover in the nonacademic personnel required for research, which means a greater demand on personnel services than occurs in other areas of a university.

Departmental Administration

Traditionally, academic departments were administered entirely by department chairmen (or heads), one or two additional faculty such as a graduate school representative, etc., occasional departmental faculty, and several secretaries. The advent of research in a large way, which means primarily sponsored research, has required a sizable expansion. A key position has been introduced: a nonfaculty administrator, who is sometimes called the departmental executive officer or the assistant to the chairman. To some extent this person may perform functions that appear similar to those in research administration, particularly in the monitoring of sponsored research projects. Many of these functions are better done at the departmental level, closer to the actual research performed; in other words, some decentralization is desirable.

Departments with large research endeavors may need other personnel also. Clerical requirements must be met. A procurement specialist to assist with specifications and even with the location of vendors can facilitate the acquisition of specialized items. Demands for secretarial and stenographic services are substantially increased by sponsored research to handle proposals, letters, reports, and manuscripts that are necessary for research. Then there are supporting services such as shops and stockrooms.

There is an in-between area in the totality of university management for research, which will be discussed as part of departmental administration because that is where the costs are generally budgeted and recorded. Faculty committees, or committees that are part faculty and part administration, play a much more important role in many universities in overall management than most persons outside of universities realize. The numbers of such committees and their concerns are legion. The concerns range through faculty appointments and promotions, policy, graduate school, library, benefits, facilities, etc. Some committees were specifically created because of sponsored research, such as a university research board and committees on equal employment opportunities, nonfaculty professional personnel, human subjects, animal care, etc. In addition to the specific functions these committees have, they provide a brake on the centrifugal force created by the widely divergent interests of those who make up a university community.

In chapter 7 and earlier in this chapter, the subject of direct versus indirect costing was discussed; if there is repetition here, it is not by mistake, but for emphasis. Departmental administration is where the problem of direct versus indirect primarily arises, and this is also true for infringements on the principle of consistency. Indirect costing of most of the functions and elements of departmental administration discussed in this section is probably the best course to follow.

Buildings and Equipment

Indirect cost computations for universities generally assume average building lives of 40 years for depreciation or 50 years for use charges. No building this old has been observed that is now actively used for experimental research unless there have been capital improvements approaching or greater than original cost. Will the same thing be said by the year 2020 or later? Will the kinds of space and the way space is outfitted and which is needed for research change as much in the years ahead as they have in the past? The answer is probably yes. *Flexibility* in the design and construction of buildings, including internal utilities and services, is the only way to minimize later regrets or costly changes.

Scientific and other specialized equipment is often paid for as a direct charge under sponsored projects. Sponsor approval may be necessary, as well as internal certification that no similar equipment is available to fill the need. Property accounting and a periodic inventory are required if the sponsor retains title or has residual rights, as discussed in chapter 3. General-purpose equipment such as office equipment and machine tools must generally be paid for by the university; funds for replacement, except for inflation effects, may be made available by accumulating a reserve based on the equipment use charge or depreciation factor in indirect costs.

Libraries

If properly funded, organized, and operated, libraries are an important asset to research, although there are significant differences in demands on libraries, depending on the field of research. The availability of books and other materials in a library provides access to existing knowledge, so that the next step can be taken further upward rather than duplicating a step already taken.

The explosion of knowledge in recent years has created major problems in financing, housing, and operating libraries. No university library can have every book or journal or other item a staff member may want, and at the time and place where the item is wanted. The time and place problem can be substantially alleviated by branch libraries that contain the books and journals most frequently requested by those in close proximity. For the most efficient use of the library system, all items in a central library and branch libraries should be centrally catalogued. Interlibrary loan systems with other institutions and public libraries can provide items not available in the university where the items are needed, and immediate computerized readout techniques are available in groups of cooperating institutions to minimize the delay in locating a needed volume.

There have been claims that some libraries do not serve university research needs and that the necessary books and journals are paid for as a direct charge out of contract and grant funds. To the extent that this may possibly be true someplace, it is a grossly ineffective and inefficient method of operation except for a large, self-contained laboratory where sufficient funds are available to pay for all the myriad items that may be needed. Nevertheless, there undoubtedly are some universities whose libraries do not adequately serve research needs. Funds can be obtained through the library element of indirect costs to help provide for those needs. Advisory committees composed of library users in various disciplines should have a voice in the acquisitions.

Shops and Stockrooms

The kinds of shops and the kinds of stockrooms provided are particularly subject to the perennial argument of centralization versus decentralization. It is argued that more efficient use can be made of personnel, facilities and equipment, and volume purchasing of stockroom items through the use of central shops and central stockrooms. The argument for decentralization is primarily based on the inescapable fact that time is money. Decentralized shops and stockrooms can be closer to the research so that access is quicker and easier. In centralized shops, furthermore, there is almost always a scheduling queue, so that the researcher must wait even if all that is needed is a little job.

There are machine shops, electronics shops, and glassblowing shops; drafting might also be classed with shops. One-at-a-time items are the regular type of output and there is no mass production, as in industry. This means, at least for central shops, that the machinists should be better than average machinists, the electronics technicians better than wiremen, and the glassblowers expert.

The author is convinced from experience that partial centralization and partial decentralization is advantageous; there is a need for both central and decentralized shops and stockrooms, and each institution is unique in its requirements. This is the most efficient way of operating when both time and money are considered. Central shops are probably better for precision, complex, sometimes multiple sorts of jobs, where detailed drawings or requirements are generally supplied. The small shop, with only a few tools and only part-time personnel, or technicians who also do shop work, is better adapted for the little jobs, with perhaps only back-of-an-envelope sketches to work with. Central stockrooms are better for providing a large variety of items, many of which are not used frequently. Local stockrooms, sometimes no more than a cabinet, are better for items needed frequently or quickly.

From an accounting standpoint, central shops are more readily charged out on the basis of hourly rates for all productive time worked, with a loading factor for supervisory salaries, equipment maintenance, vacation and sick leave, etc.; some institutions also add applicable indirect costs. For stockrooms, the inventory pricing methods of last-in-first-out or average costs are most often used; some institutions add a loading factor for stockroom personnel.

In many universities there will probably be several "central" shops and stockrooms, although specialization and demand may make it desirable to have, for example, only one glassblowing shop or one stockroom specializing in chemicals. In some universities, a particular shop or stockroom is the management responsibility of a particular department whose requirements for the services or supplies provided represent most of the total demand; such a system works if the managing department gives adequate priority to the needs of other departments. Central university management also works, and often works more effectively, if sympathetic attention is given to all users. Common costing and pricing methods for all similar shops and stockrooms are important to insure equitable charges to all users and to satisfy government auditors.

For small shops and for small stockrooms that may better be called storerooms, either of which may service individual departments or individual projects, elaborate accounting systems should not be needed, although accounting for costs in some reasonable way is necessary for government projects.

Computer Services

The use of computers in research has increased more rapidly than that of any other tool. No university with a significant volume of research can function without having a large computer available. As in the case of shops and stockrooms, the decentralization versus centralization argument is often present. If the right kind of computer system was acquired and the right kind of systems programming was installed, services can be obtained at a remote terminal as satisfactorily as at a computer center. Nevertheless, there may still be needs for stand-alone computers around a campus for those kinds of experiments in which the computer is programmed to control the experiment and to record the output. Central review of the acquisition of separate computers is desirable to avoid draining away business from the computer center and to coordinate long-range institutional computer plans and fiscal commitments.

The choice of a major computer requires careful, expert consideration. A well-qualified computer center director and staff are invaluable and expensive. In this area in particular, because of its importance to a wide segment of the whole university, competence has no substitute.

Opinions differ on whether the same computer should serve both academic and financial functions of the institution or whether there should be a separate computer for each. Both methods are used, with changes occurring once in a while from one method to another in an institution. Both have been reasonably successful in some institutions and both have been less than successful in others. In the author's opinion, the answer (if there is an answer) lies in the competence of the computer center director and staff and in the kind of computer and systems programming available. The university officer to whom the computer center director reports can have a major influence by skewing the services rendered to one or the other functions of the institution. An oversight committee composed of representatives of user groups can be helpful.

Charging for computer services is complicated in some institutions. Even the development of proper rates to charge for computer services is sometimes poorly done. Certain types of users, such as students, often have free access to a computer with a minimum of constraints. Charging to sponsored projects is waived because project funds have been exhausted, but the computer continues to be used, again without constraints. Arguments were made in the earlier days of computers for treating them as an indirect cost, as libraries are treated, freely available to all without a direct charge (the author was at that time a strong proponent). But when a $25,000-a-year project uses $200,000 a year of computer time, the library analogy breaks down.

The government rarely accepts costs for the use of *large* computers on bases other than those that charge *all* users of computer services on a consistent basis. The total of charges made during any one fiscal year does not have to equal precisely the costs for the computer during that year. Thus, during the early years of a new computer there may be an underrecovery of costs when the computer is underutilized, which is to be balanced by an overrecovery during later years when utilization is high. Costs for a computer center normally include all operating costs, depreciation if the equipment is purchased, depreciation of initial programming or software costs, plus generally applicable indirect costs. Internal nonproject use, as for instruction, may be handled on the basis of assignment of an appropriate account number, with an allocation of funds (sometimes called "funny money" because no actual dollars change hands) based on some kind of review of needs. Priority rates may be employed, with higher rates for higher priority.

Animal Centers

Much research conducted in medical centers, agricultural schools, and departments of biology, physiology, and psychology requires the use of animals. Government regulations mandate the types of accommodations and care that must be furnished for these animals, and animal care committees are often needed to comply with the regulations.

Once again the question of centralization versus decentralization arises. For animal centers, the case for centralization is strong, although more than one center may be unavoidable because of geographic separation—between a medical center and a biology department, for example. However, the requirements are just too complex to be met in a number of different animal quarters.

Charging research for animal centers on some sort of a direct utilization basis is more equitable than trying to include the expenses in indirect costs. One method is a daily charge per animal, with the charge based on the type of animal.

Occupational Safety and Health

In recent years the federal government and state governments have imposed greatly increased requirements for occupational safety and health. These infringe heavily on the performance of research, particularly experimental research. New problems constantly arise, the most recent being in research involving recombinant DNA.

No university can operate efficiently and perform a substantial volume of research without an organized approach to occupational safety and health. Attempts to charge the costs directly to research projects, except for simple identifiable items like radiation badges and waste disposal cans, do not work. Experience shows that many principal investigators will refuse the services if they must pay the costs directly. Indirect cost treatment is the only answer.

Operation and Maintenance

Operation and maintenance include the provision of utilities, maintenance, janitorial services, and noncapital improvements and renovations of buildings, together with the upkeep of grounds and exterior appurtenances. No research can be done without operation and maintenance of physical plant. As is frequently the case for other services, research needs are often different and more demanding than for instruction and other functions. Extra requirements for power, more precise temperature and humidity control, and temporary partitions are more frequently required among the special services particularly necessary for experimental research. A university that expects to have quality research performed must expect to satisfy these requirements.

9

Organization

BLENDING GOOD MANAGEMENT FOR RESEARCH INTO A UNIVERSITY IS NOT easy, due to a complex system of governance. Even in the most well-managed organizations, a person's influence is generally different from that implied by the organization chart. In a university this is probably even truer, and a person's abilities, reputation, and powers of persuasion have an even greater effect on the importance of a position occupied.

Universities have another special characteristic. In probably no other organization would one find such a large group of employees like a university faculty, who are engaged simultaneously in producing two different end products—in this case, educated students and advances in knowledge. At the same time these same employees may be engaged in management functions such as departmental actions on appointments and promotions of other faculty members, while also serving on advisory committees concerned with university policies. In addition, faculty members acting somewhat as a committee of the whole, or as a representative faculty senate, can in some ways be described as a university legislature.

It is for these reasons that a description and analysis of university organization in terms of management for research as discussed in the previous eight chapters is complicated. There are almost as many variations in organization as there are universities. What this chapter attempts to do in part is to describe the salient features of different organizational arrangements that have been encountered or are known in some other way. Also included are comments, where pertinent, regarding interaction with or fulfillment of the policies, functions, and other management aspects discussed in the previous chapters. From the standpoint of composition, research administration is a nucleus for each kind of organizational arrangement analyzed.

The remaining substance of this chapter is divided into two major parts. The first covers affiliated foundations, which have a different corporate structure for handling research administration and allied matters. The second reviews the various types of organizational structures used for research administration within the corporate body of a university itself.

Affiliated Foundations *

Affiliated foundations, as the term is used in this volume, mean separately incorporated nonprofit organizations that perform functions in connection with sponsored research carried on by their parent universities. They often perform other functions as well, such as those related to nonresearch projects, patent management for *all* inventions made, and possibly, general fund raising. All such foundations of significance that have been identified by the author are affiliated with state-supported universities, except for two that are city-supported. (Since the function is almost identical, the remaining discussion will treat all as if they were state-supported.) Many state requirements that were established (and are appropriate) for the regular state government agencies were not designed for the effective administration of sponsored research. They impede its effective and efficient carrying out of that activity. Even state officials who have acquired an understanding of the circumstances at times have encouraged the formation of separately incorporated organizations. The primary reason for the existence of these foundations is that their separate legal status makes it possible for universities to live with state legislative and administrative restrictions that would otherwise seriously hamper the performance of sponsored research and other projects.

Independent universities do not need the mechanisms of affiliated foundations because their corporate powers are sufficient to provide the necessary flexibility and other attributes required for research. State universities having a substantial degree of constitutional autonomy have many of the same characteristics as independent universities; therefore, they also rarely need affiliated foundations. These universities include a number of the top state institutions ranked in terms of total research volume.

Turning again to state universities that do have affiliated research foundations, 47 have been identified in the United States. Some were established more than 30 years ago, not originally to handle sponsored research, but whose functions have been more recently expanded. The remainder came into being rather evenly in the intervening years. Based on National Science Foundation data for fiscal year 1975, 11 of the top 50 state universities, or 22%, ranked in order of total annual research expenditures, had affiliated foundations. Ten of the next 50, or 20%, did likewise. The affiliated foundation is a significant phenomenon in management for research.

* Some of the information contained in this section is from the report "University-Connected Research Foundations: Characterization and Analysis," NSF grant NM41821 (Norman: University of Oklahoma, 1977).

The services provided by affiliated foundations to their parent universities vary widely, since such foundations range from little more than a "paper" organization with only a few employees to one that consumes a significant portion of the indirect costs reimbursed for the projects it handles. However, no matter how "complete" a foundation is in terms of the functions it performs, it still represents only a fraction of all management for research discussed in the earlier chapters. The functions performed can be examined as follows:

1. The climate for research (chapter 1) can be affected only to the extent that foundations actually take over functions that are hampered by state-imposed restrictions in areas like purchasing and subcontracting, nonfaculty personnel employment, and accounting. While these are important, the other factors discussed in that chapter far outweigh them.

2. Foundations have a minimal effect on the formulation of policies and criteria for the acceptance and performance of sponsored research, as covered by chapter 2.

3. Affiliated foundations perform major university functions in developing and implementing sponsored research. Of the functions discussed in chapter 3, except for departmental review and approval of proposals, there are very few that some foundations do not perform. For example, some even play a substantial role in proposal preparation. However, some affiliated foundations do not handle all the sponsored research of their parent institutions, for reasons so varied and often so unique to one institution that their examination here would not be of much value.

4. Affiliated foundations have little to do with organization and management of interdisciplinary research (chapter 4) except in some cases for the employment of project personnel.

5. Nonfaculty professional personnel (chapter 5) are sometimes employed by a foundation where state regulations or restrictions impose barriers.

6. The great majority of affiliated foundations handle patents and often copyrights, also (chapter 6). Patenting and licensing are rarely limited to inventions from only sponsored research, but include as well all inventions emanating from all of a university's activities. However, formulation of patent and copyright policies is a function a university generally retains, except that the foundation may have a voice in policies pertaining to its licensing of patents to industrial licensees.

7. The introduction of an affiliated foundation into the computation of indirect costs, which was the subject of chapter 7, is a complicating factor. The parent university's indirect costs for functions the foundation performs

must in some way or another be amalgamated with, or sometimes substituted for, the similar costs that the foundation has incurred. A two-tier arrangement is also possible, with the foundation indirect costs superimposed on university indirect costs from which duplicating elements have been eliminated. Foundation accounting staffs often participate in these computations and sometimes even negotiate indirect cost rates. The distribution of reimbursed indirect costs between the foundation and the university are often the subject of special agreements.

8. It was stated earlier in this book that a primary impetus for the formation of many affiliated foundations was for the performance of functions ordinarily carried on in administrative offices or as supporting services described in chapter 8. Some foundations may handle a significant part of the accounting function, particularly for direct costs, although they can never be very close to all the accounting required for direct and indirect costs incurred. Purchasing and subcontracting are major responsibilities for many, although foundations that verge on being "paper" organizations cannot do much. Some foundations employ a number of the personnel needed. However, they generally play little role in buildings and equipment, except for property accounting for government-owned items. There also appears to be little if any involvement in libraries, shops and stockrooms, computer services, animal centers, occupational safety and health, operation and maintenance, and other offices and services.

The relations between an affiliated foundation and its parent university are often complex. The board of directors of the foundation almost always has at least one university official as a member; some officers of the foundation may at the same time be officers of the university. The one or more corporate agreements existing between the foundation and the university normally cover the relationships involved and specify one or more channels of corporate communications, but there must be many more channels at all levels if the system is to work.

The affiliated foundation clearly plays an important role with regard to management for research in many universities, and many foundations perform their functions effectively. Nevertheless, two corporately separate organizations would appear to be more expensive and less efficient than one, if one could do the job without restrictive laws or regulations to impede it. Lines of responsibility and authority are inevitably more difficult to identify, both internally and with respect to sponsors; accounting and paperwork are multiplied. Responsibility for these complications is divided in varying degrees between the state government, which enacts the laws and issues the regulations, and university management, which accepts and lives with them.

Various Organizational Structures

In addition to the author's studies of organizational arrangements employed in management for research at universities of various types, both public and independent, there is one study in particular that collected more data than seem to be available from any other source. In 1973, Steinberg reported the results of questionnaires completed by 152 universities with regard to the organizational aspects of research administration.* The sample he chose seems to be fairly representative in terms of public and independent institutions and is reasonably spread through the range of annual research expenditures.

The data from Steinberg's study of particular interest here are those that reveal the frequency with which research administration reports organizationally to various university officers. However, research administration means a different collection of functions in different institutions. In some it can mean only a portion of the functions necessary for developing and implementing sponsored research as described in chapter 3. At the other end of the spectrum is an affiliated foundation performing all the functions discussed in the preceding section of this chapter. The large majority of institutions fall somewhere in between. Steinberg said that his data include affiliated foundations, and the university officer designated for reporting is the one to whom the foundation is responsible for operational purposes. The Steinberg data for all universities, not only those with affiliated foundations, are as follows in order of decreasing frequency:

Organizational Control of Research Administration

To Whom Research Administration Reports	Number of Institutions
Academic Vice President	35
President	27
Graduate Dean	22
Vice President—Research	15
Provost	12
Vice President—Finance	11
Executive Vice President	7
Vice President—Development	5
Comptroller	5
Other	13
Total	152

* Steinberg, L., *A Study of University Research Administration: Organizational* (Ann Arbor: University Microfilms, 1973).

The several kinds of arrangements listed above for supervision or control of research administration are discussed below, sometimes in combinations. It must be remembered that the office in which research administration is carried on often has responsibilities in addition to sponsored research, as for sponsored projects in education or public service, or for internally financed as well as sponsored research, or for all university patents and copyrights. Also, the same title may mean different responsibilities and authority in different universities, so that at best the following discussion will involve offices different from those assumed or ascribed.

President or chancellor, executive vice president, or provost (to the extent that the provost is a general deputy of the president) as the officer to whom research administration reports is the arrangement that occurs more frequently than any other listing (46 times). However, the author has not encountered this arrangement in any university ranking near the top in research expenditures. There are significant advantages in this arrangement, which recognizes the important role that research plays in the university, particularly where research represents a substantial share of the entire budget. The stature this arrangement provides aids significantly in outside negotiations, and relations internally are also facilitated. Research administration has direct access to an officer with the authority to act in any of the areas affecting research, as discussed in the earlier eight chapters; this can be very important. Finally, if responsibility and authority have been adequately delegated, the responsibilities of research administration in themselves justify placing the office with those responsibilities at a high level in the organization.

Academic vice president is a suitable supervisor for research administration, particularly when the latter office handles a considerable volume of sponsored educational projects in addition to research. However, the academic vice president is not apt to have much if any control over factors affecting the climate for research, indirect costs, or administrative offices and supporting services and facilities described in earlier chapters. In some institutions the authority of the academic vice president may be even more circumscribed. In other cases this office may include responsibilities and authorities similar to those of a provost.

Graduate dean, where this office has been encountered as supervisor for research administration, has often carried a title such as dean for or even vice president for graduate studies *and* research. This arrangement is particularly pertinent where graduate studies and research are closely interwoven. Interdisciplinary or interdepartmental programs with little graduate student involvement may create problems. Compared with the academic vice president, the graduate dean lacks authority over the same aspects that affect management for research. More important, the graduate dean normally has little authority over the academic departments where research is actually performed.

Vice president for research is a relatively new title in universities; the author has encountered it in several ways. Sometimes it is a line office having primarily the responsibility for oversight of generally large and often interdisciplinary research projects or institutes; this is somewhat along the lines suggested for interdisciplinary projects in chapter 4. Sometimes a vice president for research has primary responsibility for the research administration function, which means that the title should probably be vice president for research administration; in this case research administration is placed at the same level as discussed in the first category above, where it reports to senior administration. A vice president for research may have both line responsibility for large projects and staff responsibility for research administration; this can lead to schizophrenia if the two different responsibilities are not well separated. Having a vice president for research with line responsibility for research in academic departments mixes up lines of responsibility and authority.

Financial control of research administration recognizes the necessity for a close relationship between research administration and a finance and accounting office. In fact, in all the organizational arrangements examined, except possibly for some universities with affiliated foundations, there is a section in the university accounting office that handles the specialized requirements that apply to grant and contract accounting. The dividing line between responsibilities of the research administration and the accounting office may be different among universities. Sometimes research administration transfers all responsibility to the accounting office once a grant or contract has been received. It is the author's strong belief that such a transfer should not be made; reasons are set forth in chapter 3.

Sometimes, as Steinberg's data show and as the author's visits have confirmed, *all* the *identified* research administration function is performed as a part of the finance or accounting office. This has been observed more frequently in universities with a large research volume than in those with significantly less, which correlates with the observations made in chapter 3 that major research universities devote much less of their research administration effort to the development of proposals and to seeking sources of support than do institutions with lower research volumes. The development of proposals and seeking sources of support do not relate effectively to the functions of finance and accounting.

Although the financial aspects of sponsored research are important, they cannot be all-important. The fact that the arrangement mentioned above works in such distinguished universities means that their financial officers must be attuned to institutional requirements much broader than accounting and finance, and that the research administration offices under their jurisdiction are staffed with much more than accountants.

Vice president for development as the supervisor of research administration implies an entirely different sort of role. The fund-raising aspects are to be emphasized and the operational aspects minimized. Even in the fund-raising aspects, obtaining support for a sponsored project (including the development of proposals, location of sponsors, and detailed budget negotiations) is foreign to most development office operations. Relations with private foundations may be facilitated, but there is generally little in common with other sponsors, particularly government. Development offices can be of assistance, but academic departments are critical for funding. Research administration access to authority over *any* aspect of management for research, except fund raising, is second-hand at best or outside of channels. Thus, a vice president for development responsibility for research administration has little to recommend it.

Councils, boards, and committees, which are common in universities, are important managerial instruments. A score or more can be identified in many universities whose activities in whole or in part significantly affect the performance of research. Such councils, boards, and committees rarely have any operational or line responsibility for the administration of research, although one research administration office has been identified that reported to a committee.

A primary function of councils, boards, and committees that directly affects research and that occurs frequently is the allocation of university "free" money for research, as discussed in chapter 1; sometimes elaborate procedures are involved, necessitating proposals like those for sponsored projects. Policies applicable to sponsored research along the lines covered by chapter 2, or to patent policies as described in chapter 6, may be formulated, generally for adoption by a full faculty or faculty senate. Major research projects are occasionally reviewed to evaluate long-range impact, etc. There may be committees or subcommittees for patent and copyright royalty distributions, review of proposals for research involving human subjects, computer center operations, nonfaculty professional personnel, animal care, and more.

Systematic review of all research proposals, even above a reasonably high annual budget, is rare but does occur. Where it does occur, such a review is more from a policy and general university welfare point of view than it is on the basis of merit of the research proposal. President Bowen of Princeton University said, before he became president, that committees or boards that do review proposals can perform their function best not by edict, but by "revelation and review."

Multicampus Administration

Some universities or university systems conduct research on several campuses. In such cases the central university organization may include a research administration component, sometimes as an affiliated foundation. Such an arrangement can create more problems than it solves, particularly if there is insistence that all proposals, negotiations, acceptances, prior approvals, etc. must be processed through the central office. That office should be limited to matters of policy and some procedures, distribution of information on sources of funds, possible preparation of university-wide reports, and not much more. It can function reasonably effectively if branch offices with substantial autonomy are located at the various campuses to be served. Otherwise, the problems of communication at a distance can be difficult for researchers.

10

A Preferred System of Management for Research

MANY SYSTEMS OF MANAGEMENT FOR RESEARCH IN UNIVERSITIES CAN work; the proof of this statement is that they do work. There is no unique system or ideal scheme that is best for every institution. Research is but one, albeit an important one, of the primary objectives for which a university exists. Instruction, research, public service, and the dissemination of knowledge are inextricably interwoven, so that each one has an effect on the others. The external forces of research sponsors may be resisted where yielding would be damaging, but the very process of resistance affects internal policies and practices. Personality can be an important factor. Tradition as to how a university is organized and operated is powerful and resistant to change. And management as it affects research on any scale is a relatively new art, whose beginnings were only 30 years ago.

In the face of these caveats, it should be clear to most readers that the author has preferences, sometimes strong preferences, as to the policies, practices, and organizational arrangements that would provide the best management for research in *most* universities. This chapter is devoted in large part to a description and justification of what the title calls a preferred system of management for research. It must be remembered that no management, however competent, can substitute for highly qualified faculty and research staff. But such faculty and staff may not come to an institution at all, or if they do come they may not stay long, if management is deficient. To the extent that they do come and stay, their research will be hampered by less than the best management.

Research and Project Administration

As the nucleus of management whose primary functions are related to research, an office whose responsibilities include developing and implementing sponsored research as described in chapter 3 is the first candidate for attention. The responsibilities and authorities of such an office can be summarized as follows:

1. To provide advice and assistance to prospective principal investigators for the preparation of research proposals. This can be as extensive as needed, particularly with regard to budgetary aspects, so long as it does not include preparation of the proposal itself.
2. To provide advice and assistance with regard to potential sponsors of research. This should include, as needed, the provision of travel funds for principal investigators to visit prospective sponsors.
3. To review proposals that have been approved by an academic department or its equivalent for interdisciplinary research.
4. To officially transmit such proposals to sponsors except that, before transmittal, proposals should also be reviewed by a university research board (as described later in this chapter): (a) if they are for new or significantly modified research in excess of some limiting annual budget (such as $100,000 per year); (b) if they do not conform with established university policies or criteria (such as those discussed in chapter 2); or (c) if some special sponsor review requirements apply, as for human subjects research. A list of all proposals transmitted to sponsors should be submitted to the university research board at each of its meetings and the actions taken should be defended or substantiated if questions are raised.
5. To negotiate with sponsors in regard to terms, conditions, and budget of a grant or contract, coordinating with principal investigators as needed, and to represent the university in meetings of groups of universities concerned with improved terms and conditions of grants and contracts.
6. To accept officially on behalf of the university all research contracts and all research grants to the extent that acceptance is necessary, and to activate them with an administrative digest carrying a proper account number. However, any terms or conditions that do not conform to a university policy or criterion (such as a publication denial) and that cannot be eliminated through negotiation should not be accepted unless approved by the university research board. Also, any contract or grant should have legal review if it contains a legal problem for which no precedent has been established or if it exceeds a limiting annual budget (such as $500,000).
7. To monitor active research projects and to implement or see to the implementation of all sponsor requirements, including but not limited to financial status, cost transfers, reporting, property accounting, inventions and patents, copyrights, human subjects, animal care, etc.
8. To act upon or see to fulfillment of the steps necessary for proper completion or termination of all research projects.

Arguments against such a substantial delegation of authority to research administration, as described above, particularly for items 3, 4, and 6, will be heard in a number of universities. Some offices will claim that their prerogatives are being infringed on; some will claim that only they have the knowledge to review adequately a particular facet of a proposal; some will point to a minor error made with respect to some earlier project as proof that delegation of authority will not work. However, acquiescence to these arguments leads to the approval chain discussed in chapter 3, where there are so many approvals and each approver is so busy that no one catches the problem. As to mistakes, it is axiomatic that the more second-guessers there are, the less responsible the initiator feels. Too many mistakes generally mean that the person responsible is not fully qualified; the answer is not that his or her actions should be reviewed several times, but that a new head is needed.

It should be noted, with respect to proposals, that a university research board under item 4 above is to have the opportunity to question approval actions by research administration. At the very worst, then, a proposal could be withdrawn if approval is overridden.

The functions delineated in chapter 3 and discussed above can be best described with a title of "sponsored research administration." Organizationally, however, there are advantages in adding administrative responsibilities for internally financed research, i.e., research paid for from institutional "free" funds of the type discussed in chapter 1. This is not intended to imply that such an office would have any authority regarding the allocation of such funds. However, there are inevitably administrative tasks that must be performed in addition to decisions on allocations. There seems no better place to have these tasks performed than in an office having administrative responsibility for all the rest, much larger share, of university research. A single source of information on all research being conducted in an institution is of significant value; with this function added, the most descriptive title becomes "research administration."

In addition to sponsored research, there have appeared in more recent years other kinds of sponsored projects on university campuses. These include educational services, curriculum development projects, facility and equipment grants, institutional grants, and a variety of public service undertakings. The kinds of proposals required, the development of sources of support, the negotiations necessary, and the monitoring of performance are similar to the functions needed for sponsored research. Many universities have placed responsibility for these sorts of functions in the same office that handles sponsored research. Combined with the earlier functions, this leads to a title such as "research and project administration."

As stated in chapter 6, patentable inventions and copyrightable material can be primary products or outputs of university research. If a university proposes to handle these consistently, it is important that there be an administrative "home." It is logical that this home be where administrative responsibility lies for those activities giving rise to most of the patentable inventions and copyrightable material, i.e., the office with responsibility for research and project administration. Without this sort of relationship, the negotiation of patent and copyrightable conditions for sponsored projects can be seriously handicapped. After negotiation it is difficult to separate and transfer to another office the implementation of sponsor requirements on patents and copyrights. The research and project administration office should already have a close working relation with ongoing research and scholarly endeavors from which patentable inventions and copyrightable material are most apt to arise. However, assumption of this responsibility does not seem to warrant a change in office title from that suggested in the preceding paragraph.

Other responsibilities discussed in earlier chapters that should fall directly within the purview of an office of research and project administration are few. Participation in computation and negotiation of indirect cost rates, which were the subject of chapter 7, is strongly recommended, since the negotiation of many grants and contracts requires an intimate knowledge of how these rates were derived and what their composition is. Also included as a responsibility for research and project administration should be negotiation, execution, and administration of subcontracts for services or products involving research or development or of subcontracts let on a basis other than a firm fixed price (see chapter 8). Forms should be prepared and periodically revised for all regular purchase orders so as to pass on to suppliers the applicable government terms, conditions, and boilerplate; such preparation should be done with the cooperation of legal counsel.

In addition to the direct functions and responsibilities of an office of research and project administration, that office and in particular the head of that office can have a beneficial and sometimes a strong influence on all other aspects of management for research. One of the most effective ways this can be done is by participation as a full-fledged member of councils and committees whose deliberations have an important effect on research; this may logically extend to membership in a president's cabinet, if such a body exists. Another reasonable function is preparation and revision of drafts of policy statements applicable to sponsored research, as discussed in chapter 2, and to patents and copyrights, as discussed in chapter 6.

Where in the organizational framework of a university should such an office of research and project administration be placed? The preference for a university with any significant volume of sponsored activity should be clear. There should be a *vice president* or equivalent of research and project administration. The responsibilities and authorities described above fully justify such a position. Direct access is provided to the president, which extends over all other offices whose jurisdictions affect research. Prestige is a significant factor in negotiations with outside sponsors, and the same prestige carries weight internally. The necessary contractual authority urged in chapter 3 is more readily granted by a governing board to a vice president. Finally, and in some ways more important than others, someone with the capabilities required can best be attracted and retained if the position carries the title of vice president and has the commensurate salary.

University Research Board

Too many councils, committees, and boards whose jurisdictions overlap each other or overlap the jurisdictions of administrative offices can create problems in governance. With due regard for the caveats stated in the first paragraph of this chapter, a university research board having responsibility for *oversight* of *all* research activities in an institution offers many advantages.

With regard to the importance of having such a board, it has been stated that "committees (or boards) are essential in organizations dependent upon response rather than command in their effective operation." * A university is this kind of organization. A university research board brings together representatives of the faculty and administration and represents their concern with research as it fits within the total mission of the university. There is thus a balancing feature added within the organization for research, whose members do not have research as their sole or primary concern. Other reasons for having a university research board will be evident from its functions, which are listed later in this chapter.

An ideal board would be composed of about seven to a maximum of twelve members, with a preferred membership of nine or ten. A majority of the members would be senior faculty members having strong research or scholarly interests. Part might be elected and part appointed by the president, with consideration for some general representation of the disciplines involved (such as a chemist to represent natural sciences, an economist to represent social sciences, etc.). Staggered terms of office, of

* J. Douglas Brown, *The Liberal University* (New York: McGraw Hill Book Co., 1969).

several years each, would provide continuity. Ex officio administrative members should include the vice president for research and project administration, financial vice president or treasurer or controller, dean of the graduate school (except see below), and possibly more. Deans of schools can be elected (rare) or appointed members of the board.

The chairmanship of a university research board may often not require full-time effort. The rank should be that of a university dean or vice president. Because of the close relation between graduate studies and research, there is much to be said in many universities for having the dean of the graduate school act as chairman of a university research board; the provost may be a logical solution in other universities. The board should report through its chairman to the president, and be advisory to the president in the sense at least that an appeal against its decisions can be taken to him or her. The vice president for research and project administration only rarely will be an acceptable choice for chairman of a university research board, and only then if he or she has come from faculty ranks.

The functions of a university research board can be summarized as follows:

1. To advise the president with regard to any factors that significantly affect the climate for research in the university, as described in chapter 1. To allocate or recommend allocations of institutional "free" funds for research.

2. To formulate and implement policies and criteria for sponsored research of the types described in chapter 2. Some of these may properly be subject to approval by the full faculty or faculty senate before they are promulgated. However approved, they should be widely disseminated.

3. To review and approve (or disapprove after consultation with the principal investigator) proposals referred to the board by the vice president for research and project administration, as covered by item 4 of the previous section of this chapter, and to review and approve or disapprove grants and contracts referred by the vice president for research and project administration under item 6 of the preceding section.

4. To utilize the office of research and project administration to provide information and advice to implement decisions of the board and of its committees as discussed later in this chapter, and to review at each meeting lists of proposals approved by research and project administration.

5. To pay particular attention to the development and progress of interdisciplinary projects or programs. If a dean or other coordinator for interdisciplinary research is appointed, as mentioned in chapter 4, he or she could be a member of the board or could meet with the board frequently.

6. To periodically review *in person* on the site the research in progress in schools or groups of departments; without site visits it is impossible for the board to get a "feel" for the research that is underway. Interest shown in research pays off handsomely in dividends of appreciation and cooperation from those whose research is thus inspected. This is truly functioning by means of "revelation and review."

7. To participate actively with regard to nonfaculty professional personnel, as discussed in chapter 5, possibly with a special board committee.

8. To formulate and recommend patent and copyright policies for adoption by the full faculty or faculty senate, and to allocate or recommend allocation of royalty income.

9. To cooperate in the education of faculty and staff with regard to indirect costs, as covered by chapter 7, and to establish methods of cost sharing through either indirect cost reductions or other means.

10. To assay the effectiveness and make recommendations where necessary in the interests of improved research with regard to administrative offices and supporting services and facilities discussed in chapter 8.

11. To assay the effectiveness and make recommendations where necessary in the interests of improved organizational arrangements, as discussed in chapter 9.

A university research board acting alone would find it difficult to perform all the functions listed above. However, they can be accomplished if reliance is placed on a competent office of research and project administration for information, advice, and implementation, and if a sound structure of board committees is established.

Research Board Committees

A university with only a modest volume of research can adopt with salutary effect the university research board and office of research and project administration structures advocated above. However, the larger a university's research volume becomes, the more important it will be to have delegated authority and responsibility to committees of the board, so that the board may not be overloaded or become so large as to be unmanageable. In some cases also, particular expertise may be called on, because of inadequate representation on the board. A discussion of some *possible* committees of the board follows.

An institutional research fund committee or committees may be needed for the allocation of endowment or state funds that can be used for research, plus "ostensible" indirect cost reimbursements, patent or copyright income not set over to departments, institutional grant funds, etc. More than one such committee may be desirable, with each committee concerning itself with a group of disciplines. Granting jurisdiction to a single committee for all "free" research funds from whatever source, which are to be allocated to a group of departments, is strongly preferred to separate committees for each source of funds, such as institutional grants, endowment income, patent income, etc.

A committee on nonfaculty professional personnel can prepare and propose the policies and criteria applicable to such personnel throughout the institution, and can review all senior appointments, promotions, and changes in status to insure that quality is being maintained.

A committee on patents and copyrights can determine the need for and propose changes in patent and copyright policies and can establish equitable divisions of royalties where policies do not fix the amounts.

A committee or committees on special research facilities such as computers, machine shops, animal care facilities, etc. may be needed under the aegis of the university research board if research represents a large part of total usage. Where education or other uses are also significant, as may be the case with some computers, the research board should see that research needs are adequately represented.

Committees on special types of research, such as that involving human subjects or recombinant DNA, must be established to comply with federal government requirements and should cover all research of that type, no matter what the source of funds.

Multicampus Universities

The extent of centralization versus decentralization in multicampus universities varies widely. This inevitably affects the extent to which the organizational arrangements discussed above can or should be decentralized. In an area that so significantly involves *personal* relationships, as in university management for research, the author's strong preferences are against administration by remote control. *General* policies, as in chapter 2, may be common, but implementation should be local. This means that each campus with a significant volume of research would have an office of research and project administration and a university research board.

Universities with affiliated foundations have their own special corporate and organizational arrangements. Foundations can perform research and project administration functions to a greater or lesser extent, depending on the services they are organized to handle. It is dubious, however, whether they can perform all the functions earlier outlined, so that some aspects of research and project administration must be performed within the university itself. For such aspects, channels of communication and lines of authority are most important.

A university should be able to establish and use a university research board structure whether or not it has an affiliated foundation.

Final Thoughts

As stated in the introduction, university management rarely manages university research, at least in the sense that to manage means to direct. This book has tried to set forth what university management *should do* in order that research may flourish.

In the first instance, management must provide the right climate for research, which includes a large variety of ingredients ranging from suitable laws and regulations through research emphasis in faculty appointments to "free" funds for research, and a number of others. The right kind of policies and criteria will result in research that is most suitable for a university environment. An organization and procedures for developing and implementing sponsored research (which represents, on the average, 90% of all university research) are essential. Interdisciplinary research, if it is to be fostered, requires special types of understandings and arrangements.

Nonfaculty professional personnel have grown to be of significant importance wherever there is a substantial amount of research, and special personnel policies and procedures are necessary. Patentable inventions and copyrightable material are primary products of university research and must be properly handled. Indirect costs are an important component of the total costs of research that universities perform, but a component that is still too little understood. Research would be impossible without a variety of administrative offices and supporting services and facilities, but each of these needs to be properly tuned to the needs of research. Finally, the organizational arrangements for research in universities must include consideration of the best means by which that research can be advanced and encouraged.

Universities have a unique role in research, which truly advances knowledge. They can, in large part, determine their own missions, and are inherently unconstrained by the economic impetus of developing a salable end product. Advances in knowledge resulting from university research can be important steps in the ladder for the ascent of man. University management for research can either hamper or greatly assist in the achievement of this goal.